BUSES
Yearbook 1995

Edited by
Stewart J. Brown

IAN ALLAN
Publishing

Contents

First published 1994

ISBN 0 7110 2255 0

Published by Ian Allan Publishing
an imprint of Ian Allan Ltd, Terminal House, Station Approach, Shepperton, Surrey TW17 8AS; and printed by Ian Allan Printing Ltd, Coombelands House, Coombelands Lane, Addlestone, Weybridge, Surrey KT15 1HY.

Front cover: A Leyland Leopard of Fife Scottish is pictured on a Scottish Cityline express service to the Yorkshire coast.

Back cover top: SYT's reaction to growing competition in Sheffield was to buy it up. Sheaf Line started as an SYT competitor, but later became a subsidiary — attracting the attention of the Monopolies and Mergers Commission in the process. STEWART J. BROWN

Back cover bottom: A Greater Manchester PTE Metro-Scania heads towards Stalybridge on route 220.

Previous page: Glasgow's bus wars received nationwide press coverage. A smoky Strathclyde Atlantean at the head of a variety of Scottish Bus Group buses in one of the city's many traffic jams soon after deregulation in 1986. STEWART J. BROWN

Catching Up

A tale of apprenticeship

Peter Rowlands has been photographing buses for nearly 20 years – but, as he recalls here, he agonised for much of the 1970s before he really began.

Prologue: the 1960s

I would show it to you if I had it – the first bus picture I ever took. It was a Leyland Atlantean double-decker with MCW bodywork. I took it in 1966 in Kenton Road, Gosforth, approaching Newcastle's famous Town Moor. It was one of the first generation of Leyland Atlanteans, with relatively boxy bodywork (your term, not mine). I think it had those rather incongruous twin headlamps, horizontal-style, but I'm not certain because the picture no longer exists.

The black and white print, laboriously wrought on a monumental Gnome enlarger, got developer or something splashed on it long after I took it, and acquired an ugly blotch across the middle. So I chucked it out on the premise that I could always run off another. Much later, sifting through my catalogue of negatives, I found that this one had mysteriously disappeared. Isn't it always the way? So you'll just have to take my word for the fact that it ever actually existed.

But surely, I hear you saying, I have others that would serve just as well? The answer is no. That single picture was a one-off, an aberration – something quirky to display beside leafy landscapes and Victorian buildings. In those days I didn't take bus pictures. I took portraits, holiday pictures, moody street scenes, snaps.

Enlightenment: the 1970s
Peripheral vision

Nothing wrong with photographing the changing face of your city. Anyone might do it. When the 1970s dawned I was living in the West Midlands. So why not include a Park Royal-bodied Daimler Fleetline double-decker in my shot of the Bull Ring roundabout? Surely it added interest to the picture? To be honest, I'd tried this three years before, back up north. My shot of the Tyne Bridge, for instance, just happened to include

Below:
All-time favourite: a Newcastle Regent III operated on special services by the Tyne & Wear PTE.
ALL PHOTOGRAPHS BY THE AUTHOR

one of those AEC Regent III open-platform double-deckers with late Northern Coachbuilders bodywork (my favourite bus of all-time, if you want to know). I seemed to get away with it that time: no one accused me of eccentricity or excess. So now I slipped a few D9s and S23s into the corner of my shots.

I wasn't entirely convinced, though. The following year I found myself living in Wolverhampton, which was populated by amazing buses such as Guy Arabs with bodywork by Strachans, and rebuilt Fleetlines with narrow forward entrances and crazy front ends. Oh yes, I noticed these things all right; but I didn't photograph them. Not unless you count the arty shot between Arabs, featuring the funny Indian's head emblem that Guy fitted on the radiator: "Feathers in our cap". No feathers yet in mine.

Above:
Famous landmark: the giant transporter bridge puts an unusual Hartlepool Dominator in context. But was it worth it?

Personal record

In the mid-1970s, Newcastle's buses still had the same livery I remembered as a child. Cadmium yellow and cream with maroon coach lining. Then came an upset. Newcastle Transport had been absorbed into the Tyne & Wear Passenger Transport Executive, and it changed the livery, extending the cream to cover everything down to waist level. This was quite a departure from things remembered, and it seemed legitimate to record what had gone before – especially as I now lived 300 miles to the south. A celebration of my own history.

It required resolution, though. For five years I had taken no bus pictures at all. I wrote about transport for a living, often photographed vehicles into the bargain, yet for some reason the notion of photographing buses for their own sake had never occurred.

It proved more difficult than I expected. Buses don't stand still for you, do they? Not unless they're swathed in deep shadow, or lurking in some inaccessible corner. It soon dawned on me that taking bus pictures on purpose was an altogether more daunting proposition than doing it as an incidental to something else. I took about ten rather turgid colour shots, which the lab obligingly under-developed, and I felt uneasy about the whole enterprise. What was I supposed to do with ten bus pictures? Show them to my friends? Stick them in an album? More likely hide them away and think nothing more about it.

Scenic celebration

Taking a picture of a bus against the backdrop of Lincoln cathedral seemed an admirable notion, so I stood on that footbridge waiting for one to come. The trouble was, I had no decent zoom lens, and the buses were too far away. By the time they moved into my field of vision the cathedral was out of shot. From ground level the street furniture got in the way; and besides, the light wasn't really coming in the right direction.

This was an irritating puzzle. I could take pictures of buses by themselves, and I could take pictures of Lincoln cathedral; but not, it seemed, both together. Yet I'd justified the visit to myself purely on that premise. My job took me the length and breadth of the country, and seemed to offer an ideal opportunity of linking bus pictures with context. Surely no one could question such an endeavour. Could they?

I should have learned my lesson from that Lincoln day – if you can't get the picture you want you should settle for second best. Yet for some time afterwards I kept up the rather self-conscious scene-painting idea. If it was Chesterfield, the picture had to feature the crooked spire. If it was Liverpool it had to have the communication tower in it. If it was Teesside, it had to include the transporter bridge. Worthy enough aspirations, no doubt; but how many decent pictures did I pass up through accepting bad lighting, back ends and impossible angles – all in a vain attempt to justify the result to people who would never see it anyway?

Capturing fading colours

Doncaster Corporation ended its long years of bus operation with a rather admirable livery in then-modern idiom – mostly red, but with a purple waist band, upswept at the front. When the South Yorkshire Passenger Transport Executive came into being and did away with this I was deeply chagrined. I would go

Above:
Into the past: Birmingham still ran ageing half-cabs in 1977.

and photograph the old livery before it disappeared. Of course I would.

But I didn't, and I didn't, and more and more buses were painted into cream and brown. Finally, travelling back south one day, I left the A1 motorway at Doncaster and pulled up within half a mile of the junction. And waited. And all the buses were in the new livery.

Then at last, when I was ready to give up, an old flat-fronted single-decker came into view, still in the old livery. It was a Leyland Royal Tiger Cub with Roe body, then 13 years old. And what did I do? I took one shot when it was still too far away from me, and got in my car and drove straight back to London.

But the idea of celebrating liveries took hold. I would take at least one picture of a representative bus in every fleet I could encounter – especially (but not invariably) in front of a famous landmark. This seemed much more positive than merely celebrating the scene. So tentatively, slowly at first, I started to record liveries that were bound to vanish: the old Sheffield Corporation dark blue and cream, the Leeds Corporation two-tone green, the Merthyr Tydfil cream and maroon. Those I caught were often in their last gasp, but at least I got them – or some of them. And a few shots of the contemporary livery alongside them.

Trial run

West Midlands at the start of the 1970s had offered a prospect that was utterly amazing. All those open-platform Daimlers and Guys – the thin, swaying bodies, straight staircases and discrete Gardner engines. Buses with bodies like these (a batch of Daimlers) had been withdrawn from the Newcastle

fleet years before; in fact rear-entrance buses of any kind were little more than a memory where I came from. Yet here they were still numerous, large as life and busy earning a living. It was like stepping into the past.

I didn't photograph them, of course. Oh no. But I did look at them and marvel. So when, six or seven years later, I was living in London and taking my first tentative bus pictures, those Birmingham buses beckoned insistently. They were still there and still running, I knew that. And damn the justification – I was going to photograph them anyway.

Well, I did. Two pictures I got (I still hadn't learned to abandon restraint). But at least they were decent pictures, taken on a bright summer's day in 1977. The only trouble was, the place held counter-attractions. There were the ex-Midland Red Fleetlines with Alexander bodies, bizarrely painted into West Midlands PTE livery. There was the trial batch of Alexander-bodied Ailsas. There were those single-decker Fleetlines with Park Royal bodies.

I photographed these and more besides, and the veterans were reduced to two shots. But the day proved at least one thing to me: I could photograph enough buses to fill two pages of my album, and no thunderbolt descended on me. It was allowed.

Sharpening the focus

Preston Corporation in 1978 was still running an assortment of front-engined Leyland double-deckers. I

Below:
Vanishing livery: a standard Leeds bus of the 1970s, soon to acquire West Yorkshire PTE colours.

was there; I saw them, and made a gesture at photographing them. By now I was taking bus photographs routinely, diverging from planned journeys to the nearest interesting towns.

But why was there a lamp post sticking out of the roof of the exposed-radiator MCW-bodied example? Why was the St Helens-fronted version blurred – and behind railings? Worst of all, how come there was one of those extraordinary rebuilt Leyland Titans standing at the bus station, yet all I got to show for it was a distant view of its curved rear dome? Even the full-fronted Ribble Leyland, which was in the foreground of the picture, was slightly obscured by a pedestrian. Why didn't I take a second shot?

Every time you press the shutter release, somewhere in your mind a cash register notches up another 25p (or however much it is). At least, it must have done in mine. It's hard to explain how else I could have stood in a town I might not visit again for years, seeing buses that might be withdrawn next week, and yet come back with pictures that were out of focus or views that were blocked.

My excuse at the time was that I was there for some other purpose, and that time constraints had forced indecent haste. I suspect the truth is that I still didn't know quite what I was aiming for. I was a dilettante bus photographer, if you like. But history will judge.

Dawning Enlightenment

There were hundreds of RTs in London when I moved here in 1973. Four years later when I started taking bus pictures there were just a handful left. I meant to photograph them, but kept on putting it off. Surely RTs would run for ever, wouldn't they?

I nearly left it too late, finally tracking them down in remote outposts such as Northolt and Rainham. And one Saturday I made my way to the Crystal Palace terminus of the 122. The weather was deep drab, and the best shot of the day was a rear view. When I returned for a retake a few weeks later they had gone.

I got one picture of an RF single-decker in Kingston, weeks before they too disappeared; and I was lucky enough to find one of London Country's rare Strachans-bodied AEC Merlin single-deckers as well. Around the same time I made a pilgrimage to the southern deeps of Warlingham to catch a single shot of one of London Country's last RMs.

One of my prized shots of the period was of a Park Royal-bodied London Country Atlantean in the last pre-NBC green and yellow livery. Undistinguished in itself, this was the one and only bus I ever photographed in pre-NBC colours, here or anywhere else. At last I was waking up to what I was missing.

Mounting panic

One day I drove down Wilmslow Road at twilight. I seemed to see Leyland Titans every few hundred

yards. But it was too dark to photograph them, and
next time I came along they'd gone.

That discovery prompted a mounting sense of
panic. All over the country there were vanishing buses
I could be photographing and wasn't. AECs, Daimlers,
Guys, Leyland Tiger Cubs, Bristol MWs – they
crowded into my consciousness with increasing
persistence. I never made a written list, but I
formulated a notional one in my head. AEC Regents in
Canterbury, in Southampton, in Ipswich. Albion
Lowlanders in Glasgow. Daimler CVGs in Burton, in
Northampton. Dennis Lolines in Aldershot. Guy Arabs
in Chester. Leyland Titans (old-style) in Manchester,
in Eastbourne, in Barrow. Bristol FLFs all over the
place. Slowly but surely I managed to tick them off.

There were many omissions. I never saw an Exeter
Corporation bus with my own eyes, though I could
have. I never caught a Lowlander in Luton. I never
saw Reading's exposed-radiator Regents Vs, though
they ran on for many years. I never photographed a
Bristol KSW double-decker, nor a Guy Wulfrunian
(though I vividly remember seeing one in 1971).

Others I did catch, with a sense of great relief. I
also caught some of the more recent buses – models
that had seemed unremarkable, but were already
acquiring a rarity value of their own. Massey-bodied
Atlanteans at Colchester and Maidstone. Pennine-
bodied Bristol REs in Reading. Lowbridge Weymann-
bodied Atlanteans in Stoke-on-Trent.

Grimsby: the final frontier

Dusk is a sorry sight when you're bent on taking
photographs. You'll attempt miracles if tomorrow is
too late. High-speed film (ISO 1000) sometimes can
help, or you can uprate a slower film instead. Either
way you often have to accept disappointment.

In any case, neither of those possibilities occurred
to me that freezing afternoon in Grimsby. It was early
1978 and the light was low; the dark blue and cream
livery looked dull. I took a desultory rear-end shot of a
Roe-bodied Fleetline (rare in sporting a low-level
destination display), and I prepared to leave. I don't
like the cold.

Yet overriding the discomfort was a sense of an
opportunity missed. What was down that street to my
left? In spite of numb fingers I struck off to find out. I
was rewarded by a Roe-bodied Daimler CVG looming
up, and I photographed it as it passed. The result
turned out to be undistinguished, which didn't surprise

7

Left:
Lucky find: a Strachans-bodied AEC Merlin of London Country stands alongside a Routemaster coach.

Below left:
Last of the Lowlanders: Albion's none-too-successful Lowlanders were fast disappearing when this Alexander (Midland) example was photographed in Glasgow.

Right:
Regents of renown: East Kent's Regents were well-known and long-lived. A 1966 bus photographed in 1978, by then in corporate NBC colours.

Below:
Titan study: a pair of Eastbourne PD2As, capturing the final era of provincial half-cab bus operation.

me. What did was the sense of elation I'd experienced in taking it. Here was a pursuit that took precedence over creature comforts, an interest in things unknown but knowable.

It's easy to say it in retrospect, but from that moment onwards I never looked back. Photographing buses didn't need to be explained or excused; it was the chance to experience a pleasure in the hope of sharing it. My road to Damascus ended in Grimsby, and I embraced it.

Left:
Pivotal picture: a snatched shot of a Grimsby-Cleethorpes Daimler on a winter day.

Below
Rare breed: in the 1970s Dennis buses were hard to find. A Loline III tracked down in Aldershot.

Above:
Ahead of its time?: a Reading Bristol RE, one of a long line of one-person-operated single-deckers in the town.

Epilogue: the 1990s

It's a strange paradox, but the keener you become to take bus photographs, the less willing you are to press the shutter regardless. I must have taken thousands of pictures since those early days, shooting far more at each place then I ever did before. But I'm more fussy now about how I do it. If the bus is half-cloaked in deep shadow I don't take the picture. I wait. If it's going too fast to freeze the motion I let it pass with a shrug (unless it's the last passing of all time!).

But I take spare shots – plenty of them. And I don't insist obsessively on finding a distinctive background. It helps, of course, but lighting and subject matter come first.

Something care and enthusiasm can't bring back are those opportunities missed in the 1960s and early 1970s. Other people's pictures fill the gaps, but they're not the same. All those pre-NBC liveries, those corporation transports long gone: how could I have ignored them so long?

You've got to start sometime, I suppose. And I've packed a lot of pictures into the intervening years. But now, two decades later, the photographs from those apprentice days have acquired a kind of nostalgic charm. At the time it had seemed I was starting too much too late, but the urgency of that period now seems intense. Maybe catching up is an essential part of the chase.

Above:
Classic view: Southend's 1960s Titans were exposed-radiator models with Massey bodywork.

'**B**uses are the jewel in the crown of London's Transport'. Thus spake Steven Norris, the first Minister of Transport for London. His was a new post, introduced immediately after the April 1992 General Election. And while Mr Norris's acclaim in the popular press is based on his alleged ability to juggle five ladies at once (his near namesake penning these words finds one enough trouble!) the creation of this post indicated a new appreciation of the difficulties of serving London with a decent transport service. The GLC of blessed memory probably knew all about that some years ago, but there we are.

It may be one piece of good news for London's transport that it now warrants its very own minister. It is perhaps fortuitous that he has turned out to be such a

Above:
The author, having been put through a computer and laminated on to a prototype Smartcard.
ALL PHOTOGRAPHS BY THE AUTHOR

high-profile one, and it is notable that since certain revelations about his personal life, the tabloid press are out in force every time he launches a low-floor bus or has his likeness transferred by computer on to a Smartcard. Whether all this attention translates into any more coverage of London bus matters is, well, another matter. But what is encouraging is that his 'Jewel in the Crown' allusion pops up all the time. It's not just a platitude to keep the busmen happy; I think he really means it.

Well, enough of politicians. To some extent London always has been regarded as a special case. As a Northerner I used to get incensed by it. I was brought up as a staunch believer, amongst other things, that what Manchester did today the rest of the world did tomorrow and I could never understand why there was always so much emphasis on London. Anyone who still ran buses with bell ropes couldn't be taken seriously.

Have I lived on the outskirts of London for too long now? These days I find no difficulty in accepting London as a special case. I mean, I'm glad that London's buses are not to be deregulated (yes, I know; I'm supposed to add the rider: 'For the time being'.) It's just a shame HM Government led everyone quite so far up the garden path before seeing sense. And I've

not yet been given a satisfactory explanation as to why deregulation is still all right in other big cities when it won't work in London. Manchester was a jolly sight better when the buses there were still regulated. They weren't perfect by any means. And I never felt that painting them all orange was a very good idea either. But anything must be better than the mess that is Manchester's buses now. And the same can be said of many other big cities.

But the fact that London is a special case is reflected in all sorts of developments in its buses. I hear a lot of grumbles about London's buses. They're not as good as they used to be, I hear. I suppose a lot depends on what you're comparing them with. I certainly wouldn't want to go back 20 years to a

The Jewel in the Crown?

London buses ain't what they used to be. **Stephen C. Morris** reflects on recent developments in London's buses and wonders if that's such a bad thing . . .

London with lines of buses standing idle in the garage because there weren't enough crews for the Routemasters and the DMSs wouldn't go without lots of spare parts which weren't available. I certainly wouldn't exchange today's situation where management gets worried when mileage operated drops down to 96% of scheduled mileage, for the days when 60% operated was considered not too bad. And under recent government regulations, all to do with Mr Major's Citizen's Charter (I, like the government, can never work out where the apostrophe belongs in this context!), if they make a mess of it the figures are published for all to see, every four weeks.

Waiting times too have come down; when I first moved to the London area 15 years ago I remember great long waits for buses which seemed as if they would never turn up; the same I recall 10 years before as a frequent visitor. Nowadays I seem to travel more than ever before by bus in London, for a variety of reasons, and am seldom kept waiting very long for one. And you can usually depend on a vehicle of at least reasonable quality when it does turn up.

Have the buses themselves improved? Well, write me off as a terrible heretic if you like (you probably have already) but some of the modern buses on the streets of London are really rather better than many enthusiasts might credit. At least in London there is now a high proportion of buses of a reasonable age. At

Above:
Steven Norris at the wheel of a 'Jewel in the Crown'.

last the age profile of the overall fleet is looking sensible. There are Routemasters there to worsen the age profile it is true. But not as many as there were.

And most of the survivors have been refurbished,

Above:
'Jewel in the Crown'? An Optare Spectra picks its way through the taxis in Trafalgar Square.

and at least look like part of a 1990s bus fleet. At the same time Metrobuses and Titans are being phased out of service when they reach a sensible retirement age. I remember when I first moved to Shepperton being appalled at the sight which used to greet me on the tedious trundle up to Waterloo of four-year-old Metropolitans dumped in a derelict state alongside the railway line in Kingston coal yard. How on earth could that be justified? And then all those Merlins, Swifts and Fleetlines which for the most part never got into their second decade in London. The older Ms and Ts are now coming up towards 15 years old — to my

mind just about the right age to be pensioned off.

Speaking personally I think it a shame that the Ts are going much more quickly than the Ms; the Metrobus was never my idea of a passenger-friendly bus, with a ride often resembling that of a camel or a glass-fibre dinghy in a hurricane and emitting the sort of whining, groaning and burbling noises which one might expect of the designs of a certain Mr Heath Robinson. The Titan was altogether more stylish and sophisticated. When I first rode on one (I won't say where it was, but it was painted orange rather than red!) I couldn't believe a double-decker could be so quiet, and Leyland knew how to make a double-decker ride well. I like their big windows too, but it's a shame that both designs couldn't have looked a bit less functional, a bit less like shoe boxes.

How long the early Ms are kept remains to be seen. But 15 years seems like a sensible life for a heavyweight bus; not four years, nor 40 years. And compared with more modern types the Titan is now showing its age. Double-deckers can be even quieter, as Scania has shown, even if it's difficult to match the Titan ride quality these days. But given that 15 years (or so) is a sensible bus life, what a shame that so many cast-off Titans are coming back to London with other operators! Maybe the jewel is flawed after all. Although the days have gone when London Buses buys new buses in bulk — I mean by the thousand — in fact it has done much better than most operators for fleet replacements. Having so many small classes makes life more interesting both for the enthusiast and the engineer. In the latter case it also leads to a headache — but, one suspects, not a headache of the

Below:
Spectra SP20, with a Routemaster registration, on the 3 in Brixton. Behind is an Olympian

intensity caused by 2,646 London-spec Fleetlines (for it is unfair to tar all Fleetlines with the same brush, as the standard, non-London-ised product wasn't a bad bus at all), 665 Merlins and 838 Swifts (less some which went straight to London Country).

Together Titans and Metrobuses make up the biggest part of London Buses' double-deck fleet by far. But the fleet as a whole is diminishing, and the double-deck element even more so, and to it have been added 354 Olympians (of which 28, those for Bexleybus, were sold off on expiry of their contract), 39 Volvo Citybuses, with rather lavish Northern Counties bodywork, 71 Scanias (29 with Alexander bodywork, the rest Northern Counties) and 25 Optare Spectras.

Two hundred and sixty of the Olympians were London Buses' last major order for double-deckers, delivered in 1986/87, and conform in many respects to earlier London bus deliveries, but most of the more recent deliveries have a brightness and freshness to them which is certainly attractive to the passenger. Indeed the contrast between these more recent vehicles

Above:
At Ilford on the 25 is a Northern Counties-bodied Scania.

and a Routemaster, in non-refurbished form at any rate, is marked — not, it has to be said, in the Routemaster's favour. One cannot deny that by 1950s and even 1960s standards the Routemaster interior was well-designed and attractive, but in the 1990s it is getting dowdy and the comparatively small windows

Below:
Though most Greenways are for Red Arrow work, one of the prototypes, a former Crosville bus which came from North Western, is with CentreWest and is used on the 607 express service from Uxbridge to Shepherds Bush, along roads which are to feature extensive bus priorities and the Countdown passenger information system.

make for a gloomy aspect.

Much has been gained in this respect by the refurbishing exercise. Speaking to one of the London Buses subsidiary managers a few years ago, before the refurbishing project had been sanctioned, he was concerned that money was being spent on re-engining the vehicles and yet nothing was being done to make the Routemaster more attractive to the passenger. It has to be said, whether one thinks Routemasters wonderful or not, by that stage they were getting terribly tatty both inside and out. The assertion one often hears that Routemasters are a great ambassador for Britain and are what the tourist wants certainly did

not ring true at that time. They had lost their charm and become simply old and dowdy.

The refurbishing project has worked wonders. Flexible front domes have done away with disfiguring tree damage, new paint (not just slapped across existing dents) has restored the appearance, as have new grilles, even reflective number plates and new external lighting, and interiors are now up to the latest standards. Fluorescent lighting inside and in destination boxes makes them look much more inviting at night (old-fashioned bulbs may have given a 'warm, friendly glow', but were more likely in this day and age to look just that bit sinister) and the latest London Buses moquette on seats and also lower-deck sidewalls, with light laminates has given an interior which is at home on a bus of the 1990s. To the purist the Routemaster may have lost its 'authenticity'; to the passenger it is now a bus of the 1990s and looks just as much a part of the modern bus scene as does a Scania or whatever. And yet it remains the symbol of Britain for the tourist. I have been known to question the wisdom of lavishing so much money on such old buses, but I would admit the result is excellent.

As far as single-deckers are concerned London Buses has a fleet which is almost a catalogue of the current bus industry, although at the time of writing there were no single-deck Scanias on the stocks. That was set to change with the forthcoming delivery of the SLW-class low-floor ones. There are a few Leyland

Above:
Also in a non-standard livery, using a silver metallic, is an East London   Optare Delta at Stratford in the period when they ran short workings of the 25 as far as Aldgate. They are non-standard inside, having an extra entrance step and a flat floor rather than steps inside, and they have a large standee area ahead of the centre door. Overall this gives them a neat internal layout, enhanced by current London Buses standard trim.

Nationals still around, but most of the mark 2s are being given a new lease of life as Greenways. This is more radical a rebuild even than the Routemasters have received and has given what is virtually a new bus for Red Arrow work. Otherwise the full-size single-decker fleet comprises Leyland Lynxes (if you know where to look — they'd migrated to Hounslow last time I saw them), Optare Deltas, Volvo B10Bs and Dennis Lances. Throughout the industry there is a view that the modern single-decker is the way forward; more and more big fleets are regarding single-deckers as the norm and are buying double-deckers only for special duties. London never has had a large requirement for big single-deckers, and still carries big enough loads for double-deckers on many routes. However, the single-deckers it has got are now largely 'state-of-the-art' and look well. The only

drawback (unless you are one of the poor unfortunates who ends up standing, where you might have got a seat on a double-decker) is the move to modern-style moulded plastic seats with minimal padding. While interiors are bright and modern and the buses whisk you along swiftly and almost silently, it comes as a shock to sit down with a hard bump, and while vibration and bumps are cushioned very well by the bus, what remains is transmitted straight through these uncompromising seats into the passenger. True they are ergonomically shaped and support you in all the right places (assuming your right places are in the right places) but the effect is lost by the lack of cushioning.

Which brings us on to midibuses. London Buses was not an early convert to minibuses and therefore largely avoided the horrors of 16-seat Ford Transits and Freight Rover Sherpas. Rather it led the field in bigger minibuses. London Transport has tended at times to be heavy-handed in the specification of its vehicles; ideas which have worked perfectly well elsewhere have not been considered suitable for London. However, this has not always been a bad thing; when London Buses moved into minibuses it wanted doorways and internal layouts which were as close as possible to a big bus. It may seem extravagant

Above:
London Buses didn't take to the Ford Transit in the huge quantities of other operators. The last one, FS29, was a regular performer on Westlink's 602 from Feltham to Shepperton (despite the Finchley garage code!). The author was instrumental in it being replaced by Leyland Nationals — and that's another story — and inadvertently thus played a part in shaping the history of London's buses. Ian Allan's Shepperton offices make a useful vantage point.

to have so much space in a Mercedes, and to have what seems like half the nearside taken up by door. But this was a trend which has been widely picked up by other operators following pioneering work on

Below:
Selkent has found the Iveco Turbo Daily to suit its purposes for the Roundabout services in Orpington, and is now on to the second generation, with Marshall bodywork.

Above:
The Alexander-bodied Mercedes-Benz 811Ds of the MA-class were something of a trendsetter in their attempt to make a midibus into a small big bus, with full-width doors and a spacious internal layout. Steps are a bit high, though . . .

London's buses and making minibuses work. Within London Buses and LT they were always referred to as 'midibuses' (woe betide the writer who mentioned 'minibuses'!), though everyone else called them 'Hoppas'.

'Hoppas' may not be everyone's cup of tea, and in London they really went through a bit of a vogue and we've now largely come out the other side.

Perhaps the most striking in London were the Optare CityPacers, which came in in large numbers and impressed passengers by their appearance and luxury. Less charmed were the engineers, as the Volkswagen chassis was under-specified for the job. London engineers were always convinced that big, understressed components did the job much better than small ones working flat out, and the CityPacers vindicated this view.

Apart from a few excursions into Renault/Dodges and Ivecos, Mercedes and Metroriders became standard. The Mercedes has gained a good reputation as a workhorse and a poor reputation for ride quality, and here London Buses has also stolen a march by retrofitting them with air suspension at the rear. The difference is amazing. With London's spacious approach to bodywork and a decent ride they are really quite civilised.

Of course the big move in London's buses has been the Dennis Dart. The Dart was seen as the next phase of midibuses, but is being recognised increasingly as a replacement for full-size single-deckers. This is perhaps where the most spectacular investment in the fleet has come; the first with Carlyle bodywork came in 1990 and by the spring of 1994 the total in the fleet had risen to 682, with more to come.

The Carlyle bodywork on the first 168 is the most stylish; that S-shaped front, deep windscreen and bonded glass immediately mark out the bus as something different, and the interior, with big, deep windows is probably the best so far. Next came the Reeve Burgess version, later Plaxton, and this accounts for the biggest batch of Darts, nearly half the total, in both 8.5m and 9m versions.

Then came the rather quirky Wrights-bodied version. Those that have them think they're wonderful, with easily repairable and solidly-built aluminium body, but their functional lines and a front end with recessed windscreen look 30 years out of date. Was this back to the old days of engineers calling the shots and ignoring the importance of style to attract the customer back? Worthy though the Wrights Handybus body is, somehow it missed the point of the Dart.

The Reeve Burgess/Plaxton product represents the middle ground. It is not as uncompromising as the Wrights body, but it doesn't stand out from the crowd like the Carlyle.

Also carried over from the 'Hoppa' concept was the soft trim interior. Now this is all very nice and cosy on a long-distance coach. But on a service bus it gives a dark, forbidding interior and later deliveries have reverted to laminates (surprising as it may seem, a more expensive option than soft trim), although with some soft trim, including the current London Buses standard moquette on some examples, below the window line. This solution leaves the impression of a little luxury yet leaves the interior bright and airy.

I can't help thinking of the Dart as the spiritual successor to the RF. I'm not sure Wrights were right to emulate the look of the RF (at the front anyway), though I do appreciate that windscreen replacements are cheap and it's actually an aerodynamically efficient design. Well, as much as a box-like bus can be. Apparently you don't actually need the windscreen; the airflow (I'm told) is such that you could even drive one in the rain without a windscreen and not get wet. Well there's a useless fact for you.

They're about the same size as an RF (which we never thought of as anything other than full-sized at the time) and generally perform very similar duties. I don't expect they'll clock up 28 years in service like some RFs did; I doubt either that were a Dart to live that long it would be as presentable as an RF at that age. But Dennis Darts don't weigh more than the average double-decker either. I am sure the bus enthusiast in me would happily travel miles for a ride on an RF. But S. Morris the bus passenger rather

prefers the nippiness and quiet running of a Dart and the nice big windows. The seats could do with being wider and maybe the Darts accelerate — and stop — rather too quickly for comfort. But they're a fine modern bus and ride as well as anything with steel semi-elliptical suspension can be expected to. Though I often wonder why Dennis has never engineered it for air suspension. With Volvo coming up on the rails with the B6 it may need to think about it.

So much for London Buses. The London Transport tendering system has also helped to bring in plenty of new buses. Not all routes have been tendered on the basis of new buses, hence the recycled Titans referred to earlier on. Some of these look OK; London & Country's livery seems to suit most buses well and the Titans are no exception. London Coaches' ones look quite stylish. Then there is London Suburban Buses . . .

Moving swiftly on, many of the London tendered service operators have new rolling stock. Particularly favoured seem to be the Leyland/Volvo Olympian and Volvo Citybus, while the Dart has also found favour here. The Volvo B6 has also made its London debut with the independent sector. You have to know what you're looking for to tell them apart from Darts; the biggest giveaway, if you can't see the diminutive badges used generally by both manufacturers, is the longer rear overhang of the B6.

All of which means you seldom have to travel on an old bus in London. Indeed travelling elsewhere one

Below:
Quite a lot of tendered services are operated by Mercedes midibuses too, including the Frank E. Thorpe-operated Stationlink. It was launched by Steven Norris at Victoria; I think he called buses 'the Jewel in the Crown' there, too.

Left:
Dennis Darts rule OK. There are hundreds of the things in London. The 211 is an offshoot of that most famous service, the 11. A Plaxton-bodied Dart is seen in Victoria Street.

Left:
Dennis Darts rule OK. There are hundreds of the things in London. The 211 is an offshoot of that most famous service, the 11. A Plaxton-bodied Dart is seen in Victoria Street.

now finds the lack of DiPTAC provision irksome. DiPTAC hasn't just benefited the disabled; all passengers benefit, and there are few buses running in London now which don't have at least some DiPTAC features. Even the Titans and Metrobuses have had some features retrofitted, and the older London Olympians were trendsetters in having similar features before anyone much had heard of DiPTAC. Also much appreciated on the Olympians are the straight staircases, which are fitted at the expense of some seats but are so much easier to use. As people in places like Leeds, Birmingham and Salford could have told you a good long time ago.

But it's not just in having decent vehicles that the London bus system qualifies for its 'Jewel in the Crown' epithet. There has been much innovation in other aspects too. None of these in themselves have been exclusive to London, but London is probably unique in Britain in having so much bus innovation in one place.

Below:
Seen in Ballymena prior to delivery is a Wright-bodied Dart. The front end is distinctive; in the car world it would be described as 'retro'. The London connection makes one think of RFs, though I was immediately reminded of the Saro body for the Tiger Cub — especially with those ribbed side mouldings.

Above:
The RF — the Dart's grandad?

New technology has become quite a feature of the London scene. It was due to have expanded more quickly, but the Chancellor seemed to have different ideas from the redoubtable Mr Norris and chopped LT funding in the 1992 autumn statement. It was not necessarily that he doubted that London's buses were the Jewel in the Crown; he obviously doubted the value of the crown in the first place. So innovation has not spread as it should have done. But it is there.

One facet is the Countdown system on the Harrow Road. This is operated by CentreWest, one subsidiary which runs its buses by remote control. Not all of them, but already it had a vehicle location system on the controversial Gold Arrow minibus conversion of former Routemaster routes 28 and 31. This had the advantage over a roadside inspector that not only was it possible to identify a problem with the service, it was also possible to see where the problem was and use radio contact to try to do something about it.

Countdown on route 18 takes the technology one step further by telling the waiting passenger what the state of the service is, and the system has now been extended to the Uxbridge Road along with a whole series of priority measures.

London has done quite well out of the round of installing new priority measures. Throughout the country urban buses are being stifled by congestion in their efforts to move people, and the scale of congestion is even greater in London. Nowadays congestion is just as bad in many other cities as it is in London; it's just that in London it stretches so much further. There is easily the potential for a 35-mile traffic queue from, say, Romford to Heathrow. London still doesn't fare well on the bus lane front; last time I counted there were just over 50 miles of bus lanes in London compared with 125 in Paris. But there are some very useful bus priorities going in, such as the bus lane associated with the Red Route up the A1, which makes for some pretty snappy running up towards Holloway (which shows just what can be achieved when you eliminate thoughtless, selfish and illegal parking). Then there are the weird and wonderful 'pre-signals' at Shepherds Bush and Mile End which let the buses sail past the cars and then have first crack at the traffic lights. There's a long way to go, but buses in London (and everywhere else) can play a much greater part in local transport solutions if they can get round the traffic.

Other uses of new technology include the low-floor bus trials which make the buses so much more accessible to so many more passengers, and have involved 68 new buses (or will do when they're all built) designed in conjunction with LT's disabled

Above:
Cast-off Titans are still earning a crust in London. Somehow London Suburban's have a slightly more 'cast-off' look to them than the others; it may be down to the use of LT-style red round the lower-deck windows, which makes them look a bit as if the repaint never got finished.

passengers unit. It seems highly unlikely that these will be the last low-floor buses in London either. Then there is the use of Smartcards, introduced on around 200 buses in Harrow and set to spread further, which will encourage yet more off-bus sales of tickets (and less than 30% of passengers use cash on London buses as it is, which has simplified bus use and made one-person-operation so much more workable) and will also give much more precise data about bus usage.

The structure of London's buses has also helped to improve performance. Now that individual companies of about 500 buses each have much greater autonomy there has been more responsiveness to local markets and room for innovation. A new style of London bus manager has emerged, with a dynamism which simply got squashed by centralised bureaucracy in the old days. Running buses centrally in London is all very well. Yet despite the huge volume of buses one sees in central London, it is in the suburbs that London's buses do their most important work. London has been

Below:
Many of the independents invested in new buses for tendered bus operations. Kentish Bus went for Northern Counties-bodied Leyland Olympians; this one is seen in Hackney, and the sharp-eyed will know this picture is a bit of a fix, as there's a London Buses Titan just visible behind on the 22b; the picture was posed before the buses entered service in 1990.

described as a collection of villages, though those villages have spread and coagulated to create quite large towns. After all, 200 buses in Harrow equates to a bus operation the size of that in Leicester. Places like Croydon and Kingston would be very significant large towns if they were not part of a big conglomeration. Each part of London has its own particular transport needs, and 81% of London bus journeys are actually outside the central area (Zone 1). Thus more locally-accountable operators are a sensible solution.

Whether the next move — to sell all these operators off to the private sector — will be a good thing or not remains to be seen. It is an immensely complex exercise, and by the end of 1993 they had all been made free-standing units, responsible for their own assets. In April 1994 a new London Transport Buses organisation had been set up to oversee and co-ordinate London's bus operations, with the sales of the companies scheduled for completion by the end of 1994. This has reduced the level of investment in new buses in London, and all things being equal it looks likely that investment will be slow to pick up again when the privatisation process is complete.

Is London a special case then? Well, whether or not it should be, the fact that it has escaped deregulation has made it special. Few operators in the land would doubt the benefits of a modern, well-specified bus fleet. Most would say 'yes please' to the offer of low-floor buses, Countdown, Smartcards, pre-signals etc. They're by no means just a solution for London. Sadly in the rest of Britain operators have had to fight for everything. The big operators have had to fight to support the investment in their privatisation. Tendered routes have been won by undercutting the next man. Resources have had to be squandered to maintain market share.

Meanwhile the world has moved on. The Leyland National for all its virtues is yesterday's bus. People expect leading edge technology in everything from watches and video recorders to transport. And technology is there; at a price. Not the sort of price it was a few years ago, either. But only with London's

advantages of being able to concentrate on the job in hand rather than looking over its shoulder all the time has it been possible to cash in on all this development. That's not to say bus operators in London have had it all their own way. They haven't. Just look at all the garages London Buses has had to close. Just look at the number of redundancies and the worsening of conditions for London bus workers.

But for once I agree with a government politician. Buses are the 'Jewel in the Crown' of London's transport. So they should be in Manchester. And Leeds. And Sheffield. And Glasgow. Not to mention Yeovil, Scunthorpe, Little Snoring in the Marsh . . .

Left:
A Metrobus on the 18 approaches a Countdown-fitted stop.

Below::
Low-floor Dennis Lance LLW1 arrives at a gloomy Hounslow bus station on its first day in service. Note the ramp extending at the centre door.

'WAY DOWN WEST

John Aldridge takes a rove around Western National country.

Above:
A young Bristol LH makes its way along the seafront at Sennen Cove, on route to Penzance.
ALL PHOTOGRAPHS BY THE AUTHOR

If you feel like a day out by bus at modest cost, it's quite easy. You buy a Rover or Day Rider or equivalent ticket, which gives you unlimited travel for the day on an operator's services, and probably the services of neighbouring companies too, and off you go.

But it was not always so. We have the much criticised National Bus Company to thank for this facility, which it introduced with validity on all of its companies more-or-less without restriction. Since privatisation it has become rather more fragmented, though there are still some good deals available, particularly in holiday area

Before NBC, rovers were a rarity, rather than commonplace. In those times, too, the Traffic commonplace. In those times, too, the Traffic Commissioners had considerable power over fares: indeed, they approved or refused applications for fares increases. Even when rover tickets were first proposed, other operators could object on grounds of abstraction of traffic.

Abstraction, or avoiding it, was an obsession with many bus companies, and even those that did offer special facilities often hedged them with restrictions. An example of a mixed attitude with good facilities hedged in with restrictions, at least by today's standards, was to be found at the old Western National Omnibus Company. It was once a great power in the land, and at around the time of the formation of the National Bus Company had well over 900 vehicles operating from 31 depots. There were nearly 350 double-deckers in the fleet and 235 coaches. Before you jump to too many conclusions in comparing all this with the present day, it must be remembered that the fleet included all the Royal Blue express operations later hived off to National Express, and areas and vehicles that were split off later and became Southern National and North Devon Red Bus.

Despite its strict Tilling Group upbringing, which did not permit too many deviations from standard in vehicle or engineering matters, it was an interesting fleet too. The late 1960s and early 1970s were a transition period: not only were there huge numbers of Lodekkas, but there were still (at 31 December 1969, to be precise) 59 Bristol KS/KSW double-deckers in the fleet, but only ten of the then new Bristol VRT. With single-deck buses, there were some 130 of

Above:
A Bristol SUL labours its way up the hill above Sennen Cove. This bus dates from 1966, the last year of the model's production.

Below:
One of the 12 Bedford VAMs with ECW bodies in the Western National fleet heads out of Plymouth Bus Station. The vehicles were finally completed late in 1967. The chassis had been completed at the tail end of 1966, but stood for almost a year awaiting modification to the MW design of body to suit the Bedford chassis.

Bristol's first underfloor-engined model, the LS, with 43 new Bristol LHs. There were also 12 unusual ECW-bodied Bedfords, a model introduced to fill the gap (in theory) of something of reasonable capacity yet modest weight before design of the Bristol LH was completed. I say in theory, because the problems of adapting, or just bodying, the Bedfords, which were VAM5s, seemed to take so long that delivery was not that far ahead of the first LHs from Bristol.

The ECW-bodied Bedford VAMs were not unique to Western National (which had 12), as West Yorkshire Road Car and Eastern Counties each had four. No doubt ECW had problems designing a satisfactory entrance on a chassis intended to be for coach use. The gap in availability of something suitable had arisen after the Bristol SUL was dropped from production in 1966, and that model and the companion but shorter SUS, featured strongly in the Western National fleet, with some 100 bus versions (which were quite fun) and 33 coaches (which were not much fun or very nice for longer runs). SULs and SUSs also featured in a number of Tilling fleets, but they were never a common type, and many companies had none, so they helped again to make Western National a rather more interesting fleet. In those days too, considerable attention was paid to fuel consumption, so despite its hills, the company operated numerous buses with Gardner five-cylinder

Above:
A crew-operated Bristol RE crosses the River Tamar into Cornwall on the Plymouth-Looe service. These days Western National runs the route only during the summer months.

Below:
Delays in completing the VAMs meant the first Bristol LHs were not far behind. A 1968 LH leaves Penzance with an SUL in pursuit. The LH has the original shallow and flat front windscreens.

engines. All the Bristol LS buses and the later MW buses had the same engine. The SULs and SUSs had a four-cylinder Albion engine, incidentally.

The miles per gallon achieved by the use of small engines were impressive, even bearing in mind that many of the buses were working on quiet routes. On bus work the SU family achieved a fleet average of nearly 17mpg, while 30ft long LS buses managed over 15mpg on their five-cylinder engines. MWs were even better at 16mpg, with the same engine. Newer, and much longer, buses in the shape of the Bristol REs with manual transmissions were achieving nearly 13mpg on bus work, and over 13.5mpg as Royal Blue coaches. Worst, in those days, were the new VRs, doing less than 10mpg, but they would, of course, have been on the heaviest routes.

From all that you will see that Western National was a fleet of more than usual variety. So a family holiday in the West Country offered possibilities, particularly if one could spend a day looking at buses. If it was not to cost considerable sums of money by the standards of the time, then one had to opt for one of Western National's circular tour tickets: the company had no unlimited travel rovers in those days. The circular tour tickets were usually three or four different routes making a round trip back to your starting point. Each point was itemised on the special pre-printed ticket and would be clipped by the conductor in the appropriate place to make sure you did not try to make the same journey twice in the same day. The fares too were carefully calculated on some

Right:
As far as you can go: a 1955 Lodekka prepares to depart from England's most westerly point, Land's End. Behind the bus is the Land's End Hotel, and alongside it is the small garage that was acquired by Western National from the Great Western Railway in 1929; the GWR had pioneered bus services in the area.

kind of formula, based on a percentage of the total normal fares. For example, Truro-Falmouth-Helston-Camborne-Truro cost 45p in 1971. Other round trip tickets available covered Penzance-Land's End-St Ives-Penzance, while a third example was Penzance-Camborne-Helston-Penzance.

If you were a normal holidaymaker, no doubt you chose what seemed to be the most attractive seaside towns or villages, perhaps visiting one in the morning and another in the afternoon. If you were a bus enthusiast, on the other hand, you would chose places that offered the most bus variety. Newquay might be preferable to St Ives because it had more varied vehicles or services: never mind about the scenery! A route serving Camborne could be particularly interesting: the holidaymaker might wish to make a quick change of buses there, just as part of reaching somewhere else, whereas the enthusiast would want to stay longer because the higher population and the larger amount of industry there and in neighbouring Redruth meant added bus interest.

In 1971 my family stayed at Sennen Cove, on the north coast of Cornwall, not far from Land's End, and with Penzance as its nearest large town. The village was served by buses on the Penzance-Land's End service, and as Sennen Cove was a dead end they had to make a double run, in and out, or rather, down and up, from the main road. They ran along the front for a short distance, before backing into a vacant plot of

land to turn. In those days there was still a conductor to stand behind the bus (not too closely!) during the manoeuvre. The climb back to the main road was quite steep, particularly for a four- or five-cylinder engined vehicle. Then the route was operated by a mixture of single-deckers, old Bristol LSs, less old SULs and new LHs.

Although I did not realise it at the time, 1971 was a good time for such a holiday, in bus terms at least. For it was just before huge cutbacks in rural routes as the new NBC tried to put its finances in order, and reduce unremunerative mileage, unless local authorities and county councils were prepared to subsidise. On the whole they were not: the idea of council support for buses was relatively new (and unpopular) and

Below:
A smart Bristol FLF in reverse livery sweeps into Camborne Bus Station, *en route* for Newquay on the limited stop service.

Cornwall was a relatively poor county anyway. What was perhaps a pity was that Cornwall chose to cater for school travel by special buses, rather than putting pupils on subsidised stage services. So some important trunk runs just vanished within a few years. I say important, because they were generally operated on regular frequencies, and linked more important towns, but I suppose that they were not that important, or more people would have travelled on them.

Losses of some of these services over the next few years would have knocked out the possibilities of some of the round trips, because few journeys survived. Camborne-Helston, for example, came down to so few runs that it would not have been practical for the old type of circular tour. Independents of course picked up some of the pieces, though again often running a more limited number of journeys on some of the routes.

The timing of this particular holiday was even more fortuitous, in that it was taken in July 1971: some services had vanished already in the absence of county council subsidy, but a further 24 were taken off after 31 July, so my circular day trip on 13 July was just in time: there would have been fewer buses to see if I had gone in August.

My choice for that day was Truro-Falmouth-Helston-Camborne-Truro. You had to buy the ticket at the company's office before travelling, too. Even the terminal points to be used were clearly delineated on the ticket: Camborne Omnibus Station, Helston Co's Office, and Falmouth Moor, for example. The Falmouth terminus had always puzzled me, because it sounded somewhat out of town. In reality, it was not, I discovered. Not only was it conveniently in town, but adjacent to a smart set of Western National premises with buses at ground floor level and offices above.

Next time I found myself in Falmouth, some years later, the premises were up for sale and ultimately closed. Another feature of that year that vanished sooner or later was the operation of a few trunk services of Western National on a limited stop basis, using relatively modern Lodekkas painted in a reverse of the usual green livery with cream relief. Hants & Dorset and Wilts & Dorset also did this, and the buses so treated always looked something special, although internally the Western National ones had ordinary bus seats.

I will not bore you with a journey-by-journey account of the day. Suffice to say that it yielded plenty of interesting vehicles and workings and that I lingered longer in Camborne than others had. Double-deckers were much more in evidence then, though there were independents with stage services in Falmouth and Truro even before the cutbacks.

Now, of course, day rover tickets are commonplace, but you have to check your timetables carefully before

Above:
A Bristol MW parks in the goods yard at Liskeard station. It is working route 71, Liskeard railway station-Kesbrook. This service was withdrawn at the end of July 1971, just days after this picture was taken. Cornwall County Council had refused a requested £5,598 annual subsidy, a sum that would have represented 51% of the running costs.

embarking on a complicated round trip. But after the awful cuts of 1971 and later, some things have improved. The Penzance-Land's End service came down in the mid 1980s to just five runs a day in each direction, but the 1993 timetable offered ten, including some subsidised by the county council. Youth hostellers and foreign tourists have no doubt helped increase patronage.

I used the service from Penzance one morning just a few years ago: we wasted a good 10min loading at the start, as foreigner after foreigner proffered £5 and £10 notes to the driver. We lost more time in the centre of the town with more tourists and indeed had lost so much time that I was worried that I might miss my connection at Land's End, where I hoped to get an open-top Bristol VR to St Ives. The driver assured me that I would be all right: he would stop the St Ives bus if necessary, as it had to pass ours. He then proceeded to make some appalling gear changes on the hill out of Sennen, slapping the gear selector into a higher position without pausing for the revs to drop. I felt quite guilty.

We arrived at Land's End without meeting the St Ives bus *en route,* and there was just time to photograph the two buses together alongside the old Western National outstation building before boarding the open-topper for my next ride. By this time it was Cornish Busways that was written on the sides of the vehicles, but this was really just a local identity for what had become Western National Ltd, the spiritual successor to the Western National Omnibus Company of old – a smaller fleet with a shorter title to match.

The Final Frontier

The creation of Passenger Transport Executives as bus operators 25 years ago has left a legacy which affects present-day private sector bus operations.
Alan Millar investigates.

Conceived in a more corporate, planning-minded age, the PTEs were children of Barbara Castle's 1968 Transport Act which sought to provide high quality public transport in the big regional conurbations, the parts of Britain which London-based decision makers and opinion formers patronisingly dismiss as The Provinces, or worse as Up North. For the people of

Above:
GM Buses was the new name for Greater Manchester Transport from 1986. Northern Counties-bodied Atlanteans, to a development of a Selnec design, formed the backbone of the fleet. It was split in two and sold in the spring of 1994.
STEWART J. BROWN

A quarter century ago, when Neil Armstrong was making his gigantic leap for mankind on to the surface of the moon, you weren't a space age busman if you didn't harbour the ambition of working for a PTE. Like the fictional Captain Kirk, they would boldly go where no Atlantean had gone – or split its infinitives – before. They were innovative, all-powerful undertakings at the leading edge of British bus industry thinking, buying wacky, high-tech buses, running clever new services and contemplating all sorts of innovative, co-ordinated services to lure motorists out of their cars.

Oh, how fashions change. Within 20 years, their day had passed and some were seen as dinosaurs – lumbering, inefficient monsters which lagged behind the brash, new commercially-driven bus companies of the post-Ridley age.

Greater Manchester, Tyneside, Merseyside, the West Midlands, Clydeside, West and South Yorkshire, they were meant to elevate bus and rail travel on to a hitherto elusive plane. They may have fallen short of that lofty ideal but they were the organisations which, to greater or lesser degrees, welded together long-established corporation bus fleets and painted them in new liveries.

Nothing expressed that more than the orange and white colours of Selnec, Greater Manchester's wacky, space age name for its first five years. This ousted the

staid municipal reds, greens and rarer blues of its first
10 constituent fleets and spoke volumes for the
optimism of the day. In later years, as the image faded
in industrial British weather, the orange got darker,
was applied over increasing proportions of bus
bodywork and eventually was complemented by
harder wearing muddy brown. Maybe that told us
something, too.

Historic accident helped determine the sizes of
individual fleets as did their relative success in buying
up neighbouring operators. So Greater Manchester and
West Midlands, with a greater concentration of
municipal buses on their patches and bits of the
National Bus Company and independents willing to
sell out to them, grew big and dominated their markets
with fleets of 3,000 buses apiece. Others persuaded
NBC to operate services to PTE requirements and – in
the cases of West Yorkshire and Tyne & Wear – in
PTE liveries.

In Greater Glasgow it was all very different. Long
running mutual suspicion and a surfeit of buses
chasing a declining population produced almost the
opposite effect. Had PTE and Scottish Bus Group
actually thrown pots of paint at each other's buses, the
barely hidden hostility would have been no stronger.
Years of manoeuvres to arrive at a co-ordinated
network were just that. Only manoeuvres.

The undoing of the PTEs probably began when
English local government was reformed in 1974 and
the West and South Yorkshire PTEs were created.
Control of the others passed from passenger transport
authorities (PTAs) to the transport committees of the
newly created metropolitan counties of Greater
Manchester, Merseyside, West Midlands and Tyne &
Wear. Greater Glasgow came under the huge
Strathclyde regional council the following year when
Scottish local government was reformed. The PTAs'
members were mainly nominees of local authorities in
their areas, without a political powerbase on the PTAs
and often malleable in the hands of the PTEs'
executives who could set much of the agenda. The
new committees were entirely political. They could
call the shots and use the PTEs as instruments of
social policy. If they wore a different colour from the
Westminster government of the day, they did that with
added relish.

This could happen in little ways like demanding
bus services at frequencies or to destinations which
maybe didn't make much commercial sense, but
which answered constituents' lobbying. And it
happened in a big way where fares were subsidised to
generate extra demand. South Yorkshire wasn't the
only authority to do this, but its fares policy was the
most ambitious. By the mid-1980s it was pouring £60
million a year into keeping fares at 1975 levels and
was opening up big, plush new garages to
accommodate the extra new buses it needed to handle
steadily increasing custom. It still employed
conductors and the political dimension was reinforced
by the appointment of a former Labour government
minister, Albert Booth, to the PTE's top management

team a short time after he lost his Barrow-in-Furness seat at the 1983 general election.

Measured against the relentless decline in national public transport patronage since the early 1950s South Yorkshire, West Midlands and some of the others were highly successful. But not from the perspective of the Thatcher government. Had this just been the policy of one or two maverick metropolitan counties, it might not have been bothered, but its real *bête noire*, Ken Livingstone's radical left-wing Greater London Council, was making highly effective political waves with just such a policy in London. When a court judgment against the GLC exposed the inadequacy of legislation governing fares subsidies, the government felt compelled to heed the voices of Conservative-voting business ratepayers in South Yorkshire in particular and take action.

Rightly or wrongly, those ratepayers believed they were bearing the bulk of the cost of the subsidies and that they were deriving little benefit from them. First

Below:
Minibuses flooded on to the streets of Greater Manchester as GM Buses locked horns with United Transport's Bee Line Buzz. Most were Dodges with Northern Counties bodies.
ALAN MILLAR

by cash limits, then by rate capping – forerunners of the poll tax – the councils' ability to fund the subsidies was curbed. By 1986, the six metropolitan counties and the GLC had been abolished and political control of the PTEs reverted to PTAs. But the upheaval wasn't finished.

As architect of the 1985 Transport Act, the late Nicholas Ridley was no friend of co-ordination and planning. A free marketeer, he saw little need for much regulatory control in any area of life and the PTEs were ready to be blown out of the water. Their planning role would be changed largely to a shopping expedition, buying in the socially necessary bus services that the market couldn't provide, but at the lowest possible price. Their bus operating role would go to a new animal, the PTC or public transport company. They would be owned by the PTAs, but operate as commercial companies running commercial bus routes in competition with all-comers and bidding to provide supported routes.

Curiously, while Ridley ordered dissolution and privatisation of NBC, he stopped short of putting the PTCs on the market. The government gave itself powers to break them into smaller units, but privatisation was left to the discretion of the PTAs. It was an omission which would lead to an extremely protracted disposal programme, to a great deal of

Above:
Yorkshire Rider consolidated its position in West Yorkshire by taking over — in stages — former NBC operations. It may carry Yorkshire Coastliner livery, but the Yorkshire Rider fleet number alongside the destination display on this Olympian gives the game away. The location is Huddersfield; the year 1990.
STEWART J. BROWN

confusion, much coercion on the part of government and no end of political posturing from the different perspectives of both sides.

But all that lay ahead in 1986, when the PTCs formed themselves ready for deregulation. They gave themselves new names: Greater Manchester Buses (or GM Buses), West Midlands Travel, Merseybus, Strathclyde Buses, South Yorkshire's Transport (or SYT), Yorkshire Rider (in West Yorkshire) and – most different of all – Busways Travel Services in Tyne & Wear. Liveries were played around with to greater or lesser degrees and the PTEs went through a distancing exercise with their past, too. West Yorkshire called itself Metro, Merseyside changed to Merseytravel and West Midlands went for Centro with green and yellow house colours in place of the blue of old.

Getting ready for deregulation meant adjusting overnight to the loss of massive subsidies. Jobs went, fleets were cut, fares went up, services were axed, garages closed and operating practices turned on their heads. Not surprisingly, such a drastic change was effected more successfully in some areas than in others. Where human beings are pushed into changes they might otherwise have approached more gradually, if at all, errors of judgement are inevitable and excusable.

South Yorkshire's fares freeze ended in one swift blow in April 1986 when fares rose by 250% and patronage fell by 25%. Opponents of deregulation still quote this as one of its biggest faults. No operator changed as dramatically as GM Buses which cut its fleet from 2,500 at the end of PTE operations to just 1,700, closed three garages and four central workshops and shed 2,400 jobs. In the process, it purged itself of its Leyland Titans, early Metrobuses and vast numbers of Atlanteans, Fleetlines and Nationals which it off-loaded in a joint venture with the Kirkby dealership.

This was a one-off opportunity to sell non-standard or expensive buses from other fleets, too. Merseybus ducked out of taking Merseyside's last Bristol VRTs and REs and instead of taking over the leases on 42 Olympians and 10 Metrobuses, Yorkshire Rider let West Yorkshire PTE pay off the outstanding debt and

put the buses up for sale. Rider's subsequent bid to buy them was beaten by a dealer which sold them on to eager buyers around the country – including London Buses, Stevensons of Uttoxeter and Cambus – and instead Rider took 76 of the surplus Manchester 'deckers from Kirkby.

Some of the surplus buses turned up closer to home than their former owners maybe realised. You didn't have to travel far around Greater Manchester before finding the likes of Finglands of Rusholme, Wall's of Northenden or Stott's of Oldham running ex-GMT buses on new routes. And someone at Merseyside helped Fareway of Kirkby – set up by ex-PTE drivers – pick a decent batch of stored VRTs to start its

Above:
SYT ran Britain's biggest fleet of Dennis Dominators. An Andrews Fleetline edges into Rotherham bus station, running in competition with SYT.
ALAN MILLAR

services. Fareway also exploited the sheer panic shown by Merseybus when it had axed the old route network so severely that obvious opportunities presented themselves to a new operator.

The problem for the PTCs was that, like operators everywhere, they had no idea of how much competition would arise in 1986 or early 1987, when the last gloves came off deregulation. With ex-NBC companies going through their own trauma of privatisation, they weren't yet prepared for the full fight and new and small operators were a while coming on to the scene. The one competitor which seemed to promise most of a fight tuned out to be a damp squib. The BET group was planning a comeback into UK bus operation with minibuses which were to be thrown into the conurbations. It unleashed 225 Bee Line Buzz minis into south Manchester in January 1987, planned its second assult against Yorkshire Rider in Leeds and Bradford, but was beaten to the start by Rider which put 82 of its own minibuses on the road and left BET limping off to Preston instead where it set up a smaller scale operation branded Zippy. Before the end of 1988, BET had sold out to Ribble and was out of the bus industry.

In Glasgow, the years of SBG/PTE rivalry

concluded with the mother of all bus wars. Convinced of its ability to drive Strathclyde Buses out of business, SBG threw ex-London Routemasters, new minibuses and a host of other buses on to cross-city routes and triumphantly issued a half-mocking, half-serious Christmas tape to the tune of *Ghost Riders in the Sky* in which it likened its eager managers to the Red Indians surrounding and defeating General Custer at the Battle of Little Big Horn. It cast itself in the wrong role. While television screens all over Europe filled with images of Glasgow streets gridlocked by queues of slow-moving empty buses, Strathclyde was hitting back cost effectively beyond the city boundaries and ended up winning the day and even supplanting SBG's Kelvin Central as the main operator in East Kilbride new town. This may have been Custer's Last Stand, but Strathclyde wasn't Custer.

Ex-employees and other new start businesses turned out to be among the most potent competitors in other areas. Fareway grew up to be one of the biggest operators in Liverpool and inspired other ex-employees of the PTE to set up Liver Line on routes to the south of the city. A boardroom split led to Liverbus coming on the scene a little later. Several new start businesses in Greater Manchester were set up by GMT managers and drivers.

In South Yorkshire, 20 drivers set up Sheaf Line and five managers formed Yorkshire Terrier. On top of that, the Andrews driving school branched into local bus operation and two ex-NBC operators entered the

Above:
**New to Alexander (Midland) in 1967, this Fleetline was
wearing its age well when running in Sheffield for
Andrews in 1990. The Andrews operation was
purchased by Yorkshire Traction, but was retained as a
separate subsidiary.**
STEWART J. BROWN

fray; West Riding set up Sheffield & District and ATL
Holdings, the new and short-lived owner of National
Travel (East) renamed it SUT (for Sheffield United
Transport – reviving the initials of Sheffield United
Tours of old). Their impact was particularly telling
because railway ownership in municipal days had kept
most company buses out of Sheffield and the PTE had
bought up eight of the 11 independents serving the
area before deregulation.

Here, the PTC's solution was to buy up its
competitors. By the end of 1989, it had bought up
Sheffield & District, Sheaf Line and SUT along with
some smaller operators and amalgamated most of
them into a 120-vehicle low cost operation branded
Sheaf Line. ATL had sold SUT and other parts of its
shrunken group to National Express which was fast
baling out of non-coach activities. Andrews later sold
out to Yorkshire Traction, but SYT's actions got it
into deep trouble with the Monopolies and Mergers
Commission and the Department of Trade and
Industry which ordered SYT the following year to sell
the company off to restore competition to the Sheffield
bus market.

By this time, Yorkshire Terrier had grown bigger,
Sheffield Omnibus had appeared on the scene in a
fairly big way and the competition was as intense as it
had been before SYT had gone on its buying spree.
And queues of competing buses were blocking the city
centre just as they had in Glasgow four years earlier.
SYT took the DTI to court, lost at the final stage but
ended up persuading the government to back down in
1993 and let it keep Sheaf Line.

Busways, already dwarfed by ex-NBC neighbours,
faced head-to-head competition on some of its busiest
routes in Newcastle when the Tyne & Wear Omnibus
Company – TWOC to its friends and foes – took to the
road in August 1987 with 40 high-floor secondhand
single-deckers, mainly ex-NBC Bristol LHs. This was
an offshoot of Trimdon Motor Services which was
also battling against established operators on Teesside
and in County Durham. TWOC competed aggressively
for tendered services and within two years had
doubled its fleet. Trimdon sold TWOC to Go Ahead
Northern in November 1989, but to Trimdon's horror,

the new owner sold it on to Busways within minutes, Busways sold off most of the fleet, made many of the staff redundant and added the TWOC name to its growing portfolio of small scale trading units, but only for a handful of minibuses. By then, Busways had joined the private sector.

The road to privatisation was peppered by pragmatism and dogma. Few, if any, PTAs wanted to sell their bus companies, but some recognised the apparent inevitability of it all, wanted to secure the best possible deal for their employees and pressed ahead with sales which could be more on their terms

than later deals would be as the government focused in on the remaining unsold companies. They also wanted to get realistic prices for the companies. By any standards, most NBC companies had been sold for a song, with huge profits being made by selling on unnecessary property, but neither the PTAs nor the

Department of Transport were prepared to let that happen to the PTCs.

Yorkshire Rider got in first with a landmark deal which set the standard most other PTCs would try to follow. In what then was the highest price paid for a privatised bus company, a team of eight managers and the 3,500 employees paid £23 million in October 1987 for the company's 1,165 buses. Rider brought the American concept of an Employee Share Ownership Plan (ESOP) to the UK bus industry, with the

Above:
Initially West Midlands Travel simply applied new fleetnames to buses in the old PTE livery. But a new identity was quickly evolved, using a brighter shade of blue with silver relief. An East Lancs-bodied Fleetline loads in Coventry.
STEWART J. BROWN

Below:
Yorkshire Rider is actively promoting high standards in public transport. New vehicles have included Volvo B10Bs with Alexander Strider bodies.
STEWART J. BROWN

managers owning 51% of the company, the ESOP trust the remaining 49%. When Busways was sold in May 1989, the structure was very similar and the 600 buses went for £14.35 million.

They were the most willingly sold companies. Other PTAs were playing for time, hoping for the return of a Labour government at the 1992 election and letting the DOT make the running. Two games were being played in Whitehall. One was to threaten to use the 1985 Act's powers to break the surviving PTCs into smaller units and the other was to hint that sale proceeds could be poured into long cherished capital investment plans like Sheffield's Supertram and the Midlands Metro. In Greater Manchester, GM Buses was in the grip of the PTA, with a PTA nominee as its non-executive chair and every sign of the politicians being dug in for a long fight while the number of competitors battling against it had grown to 33 a year after deregulation and would soon more than double.

By the time West Midlands Travel was sold in December 1991, the stakes had been raised. Its 1,750 buses dominated the region and the highly successful Travelcard launched nearly 20 years earlier was a major factor behind the customer loyalty which propped up WMT's market share. This was one of the big earning bus companies and it was being sold, like Yorkshire Rider and Busways, in a closed deal between the PTA and management and employees. A price of £60 million was being mooted, but Stagecoach let it be known that it was prepared to offer well over £80 million for the company. In the end, the closed deal went through, but the price was pushed up to a record £70.7 million and WMT was ordered to participate in an all-operator bus Travelcard in addition to its own. Its ESOP trust held 93% of shares in the company.

Stagecoach played a similar game when Strathclyde Buses was being sold and helped ensure that the final price paid, in February 1993, by employees and managers for its 800 buses was £30.06 million. Employees got 80% of the business and the final price was also determined by the value of 52 Leyland Olympians ordered to replace much older buses destroyed in a fire the previous year.

In total contrast, Merseybus went for buttons. Liverpool's reputation for colourful industrial relations and militant politics combined with the company's heavy, if reducing, losses to ensure that even if it was offered for sale on the open market, no one would rush to write big cheques to buy it. When the deal went through just before Christmas 1992, the company's 2,800 employees and managers all had an equal stake in the 950-vehicle business and bought it for the princely – or more likely, pauperish – nominal sum of £1. They also took on £5.9 million worth of pension commitments which were to be repaid over 15 years. Merseybus may have had bigger problems than the other PTCs, but it wasn't saddled with huge acquisition debts which, in the case of WMT, halted its

Above:
The West Yorkshire PTE sold off modern Olympians and Metrobuses in 1986. They soon found new homes. Stevensons of Uttoxeter bought this Alexander-bodied Metrobus.
ALAN MILLAR

hitherto ambitious fleet renewal programme.

SYT's road to privatisation was delayed by the deliberations over Sheaf Line, but with that finally out of the way, it could go ahead with a closed deal which had already been approved by the government even though it was insisting on open market sales for all companies put up for sale from the beginning of 1993.

Local authorities were being encouraged to push through sales by the end of the year so they could hang on to all, rather than just half, of the receipts for capital investment which, in South Yorkshire, meant Supertram which was already being built. SYT had already adopted Mainline as a new fleetname and SYT was dropped from the company's name before the 800-vehicle fleet was sold in November 1993. The 2,200 employees paid only £1 million for the company, its goodwill and about half of the fleet, but over 20 years they would pay about £40 million to rent the rest of the fleet and the garages from a PTA-owned company.

Several of the privatised PTCs gave themselves low cost subsidiaries to help them compete for tendered routes and meet commercial service competitors. If Busways didn't invent the concept, it certainly was the keenest advocate of the idea. It set up Blue Bus Services in Newcastle (reinventing the old Corporation livery), Economic in South Shields (bought by the PTE in 1975 and revived by it a year ahead of deregulation) and Favourite in Co Durham and added TWOC when it was taken over. Merseybus set up Merseyrider in Liverpool and St Helens Rider in St Helens, but relaunched its entire St Helens operation in November 1993 – complete with 20% of

staff on low cost terms and conditions – as Lancashire Travel.

Strathclyde launched GCT (initials of Glasgow Corporation Transport) in quasi Glasgow green and yellow, but insisted this was a 'recruitment arm' rather than a low cost company. All new staff started with GCT before being promoted to the main fleet if they lasted the course; it sounded better than low cost, but the effect was the same. GCT took over some commercial services from the by-now-privatised Kelvin Central which, in turn, had bought them from Stagecoach in 1992 when it was trying to bid for Strathclyde. And Strathclyde and former rivals Kelvin Central and Clydeside 2000 ended up swapping routes and establishing Strathclyde in a more dominant position in Glasgow than it had been before deregulation.

Most of the others embarked on acquisition trails, buying up competitors or expanding their territories. Yorkshire Rider benefited from the AJS Group's steady disintegration. AJS had bought West Yorkshire Road Car from NBC in August 1987, split it into smaller units and began selling it off two years later. Rider managers had a good working relationship with AJS colleagues and fixed a £3.2 million deal to buy the 123 buses operated in Leeds, Bradford and Otley in July 1989. Only a year later, AJS's York operations (York City & District and Target Travel) were bought up for less than £1 million along with their principal competitor, Reynard Buses (a successor to the old York Pullman company) to form what eventually became the 80-vehicle Rider York subsidiary.

The former managing director at York, Nigel Jolliffe, had quit AJS and set up Quickstep Travel in February 1991, running well presented ageing Leyland Nationals in Leeds; he sold out to Rider in October 1993, getting £500,000 for the 17-vehicle company which kept its identity. He kept his job and Quickstep looked set to get some newer buses it couldn't otherwise afford. Rider also had its eye on other acquisition opportunities and had even had an unsuccessful bash at bidding for some London Transport contracts.

History almost repeated itself in August 1993 when Busways acquired 80% of the shares in Welcome Passenger Services of Gateshead, took over its 38 nearly new midibuses and added another brand to its portfolio. Welcome was TWOC reborn, set up nearly two years earlier by former TWOC managers who mounted a high quality challenge to Busways, but couldn't generate sufficient profit to keep going as an independent business. In the West Midlands, WMT took over the collapsed Tame Valley company in March 1992 and promptly closed it down and the following year bought a stake in Metrowest of Coseley, which ran about 40 buses around Dudley and Wolverhampton.

Merseybus used its new found freedom to expand. Fareway and its 70 buses were taken over in April

1993 for about £1 million, retaining the identity and two founder directors. Merseybus bid unsuccessfully for Lancaster City Transport, but bought the independent Heysham Travel company instead and used it to bid for tendered bus routes. Plans to buy the Rochdale end of Bee Line Buzz from British Bus foundered, but it set up its own Manchester operation instead, adding to GM Buses' considerable woes and provoking a minor bus war in Liverpool, where GMB already ran services inherited from Wigan Corporation and Lancashire United.

By this time, Greater Manchester PTA's intransigence seemed to have got it the result it wanted least. Having blocked any suggestion of a voluntary employee/management buy-out, it had left the way open for the government to order the division of GMB in two from September 1993 and the sale of the two 900-vehicle North and 700-vehicle South companies on the open market. GMB's chief executive Alan Westwell – who had headed the Strathclyde team which saw off SBG and had axed a great deal of cost out of GMB – and his deputy went to the North company where an employee buy-out bid was fronted by engineering union general secretary Gavin Laird.

But both companies were virtually under siege. Two of the big three groups, Stagecoach and British Bus, already had substantial interests in the area, Stagecoach to the north with Ribble, British Bus to the south and west with North Western, Midland Red North and Bee Line Buses which it had bought from Stagecoach in 1989. Their dream ticket outcome was for Stagecoach to buy the South company, British Bus the North; to the PTA, which saw the private groups in terms of the devil incarnate, that dream was a nightmare which they tried to block by the terms of the sale. When preferred bidders were announced in

November 1993, half of the PTA's nightmare came true: an £18 million employee bid was top for the South company, but British Bus, which stood to gain 80% of the Wigan market, beat four others with a £29 million offer for the North company. But after much wheeling and dealing the North company, like the South company, was sold to its employees.

But others were waiting in the wings, either moving in for the kill or preying on the carcass of GMB. EYMS bought Finglands and Lynton Travel (owner of County Bus in Harlow) bought Citibus of Chadderton. Merseybus was stirring the pot, Timeline (Shearings' former bus operations) and the long-established but much expanded Mayne's had substantial operations and there was a multiplicity of others competing with everything from Routemasters to Olympians, Leopards to Seddon Pennine VIIs. The Didsbury corridor alone had a dozen operators vying for traffic and the range of operators was greater and more colourful than in the days before the PTE came on the scene and swallowed up the old municipals. On previous form, new owners of the GMB companies would have a lot of acquiring to do.

Hardly what was envisaged back in the sixties when the PTEs were created, but despite the space age science fiction, no one had cracked time travel. They embarked on a journey into the unknown and so have their successor companies. So don't be surprised if someone, someday reinvents them. Truth is often stranger than fiction. Even science fiction.

Bottom:
Strathclyde maintained a high level of investment in new buses. Major purchases included 95 Volvo Citybuses with Alexander bodywork.
STEWART J. BROWN

Is There Life After Carron House?

Asks **Gavin Booth**, looking at what has happened to the former Scottish Bus Group companies since privatisation.

We thought we'd got away with it. Although the privatisation of the National Bus Company had been completed in April 1988, there had been no mention of a similar fate for the Scottish Bus Group, and those of us who worked at the SBG head office in Edinburgh, Carron House, went around convincing each other that we had escaped the Thatcherite obsession with privatisation and would continue as before. Well, maybe we wanted to think that; secretly we were dusting off our CVs for a day that, deep down, we all knew would come.

It was different out in the SBG companies. While the end of SBG would mean the end of any need for a central organisation, for the managers of the 11 operating companies the possibility of privatisation brought with it the opportunity to buy their own companies, perhaps to make money on the scale of some of the NBC managers, if the rumours were correct. Of course there was at least an equal danger

Below:
In state ownership the Scottish Bus Group companies followed a much less rigid vehicle policy than their southern Tilling/NBC counterparts. Central SMT built up a fleet of Dennises in the 1980s. A 1981 Dominator is seen in Glasgow soon after entering service. It has Alexander RL bodywork.
STEWART J. BROWN

that their companies could be sold to an outside bidder who might immediately dispense with the old guard, but just as we at Carron House chose to ignore the possibility of privatisation, our colleagues in the companies were blotting out any possibility of defeat in the likely battle for control of their companies.

It was important to think positively. We had observed the NBC privatisation and knew the dangers.

We read *Bus Business* thoroughly every fortnight and learned of the divisive and (allegedly) devious tactics that some ambitious bidders adopted. And we saw the serious effect on staff morale that a long-drawn-out sale could have.

Of course SBG privatisation was inevitable in the political climate of the time. The first indication was given by Scottish Secretary, Malcolm Rifkind, in January 1988 when he announced that the process would go ahead, and so the Group's campaign to privatise as a single entity moved up a notch. It was a futile campaign, of course, but we all knew that we couldn't give up without a fight. There was apparent support for SBG's efforts from the Group companies, but some at least were beginning to lay their plans to buy their companies. As Barry Norman denies he has ever said: 'and why not?'

The size and shape of SBG had altered greatly over the years. The four companies that emerged by growth and acquisition as the SMT group in the 1930s, SMT,

Alexanders, Central SMT and Western SMT, covered much of Scotland from the English border to Inverness, with a major concentration in the populous central belt. These were Scotland's rural and interurban operators, but with urban networks in important towns like Ayr, Dunfermline, Falkirk, Kilmarnock, Kirkcaldy, Motherwell, Perth and Stirling.

After World War 2 the group, with a substantial railway shareholding, found itself partially state-owned when British Railways was created in 1948, and chose to sell its privately-owned shares to the British Transport Commission. The Scottish Omnibuses group, later to become the Scottish Bus Group, continued to grow, with the transfer of the Tilling-owned Caledonian company in 1949 and the formation of Highland Omnibuses in 1952 to bring together various operators in the north of Scotland. The giant 1,900-bus Alexander empire was split into three separate companies, Fife, Midland and Northern, in 1961 based on what had previously been divisions of the Falkirk-based company.

The seven-company structure (Central, Eastern, Fife, Highland, Midland, Northern, Western) was to last for the greater part of SBG's existence. (Eastern Scottish was the fleetname adopted in 1964 for Scottish Omnibuses, formerly SMT, the Edinburgh-based company.)

The only significant change to this came in 1985 when SBG created smaller companies by sub-dividing the existing units to create more market-responsive companies in preparation for deregulation in 1986.

The biggest changes affected the Glasgow area. Anticipating major competition from Strathclyde Buses, new locally-based companies were set up to operate local services where previously these had been managed from more distant towns. The Western company lost its northern part to 334-bus Clydeside; Eastern and Midland's Glasgow area operations went to 380-bus Kelvin. Eastern also lost its Borders operations to 104-bus Lowland; and Midland's Perthshire and Northern's Angus operations went to 126-bus Strathtay. This left Western with 317 buses, Eastern with 367, Midland with 292, and Northern with 254. Central (474), Fife (300) and Highland (208) escaped virtually unscathed. Two other companies were formed at this time: Scottish Citylink, which had been a trading name for the group's express operations, became a separate SBG company, and SBG Engineering took over most of the group's central workshops.

So there were 13 companies in place, anxiously awaiting starter's orders. Privatisation was going to happen, but how? What would the rules be?

It was clear that lessons were being learned from the NBC process. There would be no bargains. There would be a strict control on the number of purchases by any bidder. There would be a slight 'inside track' for company bidders. A degree of employee involvement would be required to guard against the management-domination of all but a mere handful of the sales to incumbent teams.

And so it was. The privatisation 'rules' were published early in 1990 and the complex process began. Sale prospectuses were prepared centrally for issue to interested parties. The companies met financial and legal advisers to construct their bids. The

companies were advertised at intervals during 1990 and 1991, but not before a further change was made to the company structure. The Clydeside and Kelvin companies which had been heavily involved in the Glasgow 'bus wars' were disbanded. Clydeside went back to its parent, Western, and Kelvin was linked with Central to create Kelvin Central Buses.

Strathtay was expected to be the first on the market, but the sudden departure of the managing director to join the Stagecoach camp meant that Lowland was moved to the head of the queue. As with all the SBG sales, Lowland attracted a great deal of interest from other companies, but typically several of these dropped out before the process reached the stage of serious offers.

Lowland went to its management and employees, as had been widely predicted the first sale would, in August 1990, and in successive months Citylink, Eastern, Midland, Kelvin Central, Northern, Strathtay, Fife, Highland and Western were sold, the process finishing in October 1991. Citylink, Eastern, Kelvin Central and Western went to their management/employee teams. GRT Holdings got Midland, Stagecoach got its two with Northern and (after a struggle) Fife, Yorkshire Traction got

Strathtay, and Highland went to a consortium of Citylink owners Clansman and local operator Rapsons. SBG Engineering was not sold but was closed down and the central workshops returned to the parent companies.

Since the privatisation was completed in 1991 the fortunes of the former SBG companies have been mixed. They all faced similar problems: a country in recession; high interest rates; ageing bus fleets; competition from new and established operators.

A moratorium on new bus purchases in the privatisation period meant that fleets that would normally have expected to replace up to 10% of their vehicles each year had received few new buses since 1987. As a result, elderly Leyland Leopards and Seddon Pennines with Alexander Y-type bodies – the SBG workhorses – were forced to soldier on in front-line service. It was the same for the double-deck equivalents, typically Daimler Fleetlines dating from the mid-1970s, but at least in the companies now owned by the larger groups, help was at hand.

It is worth looking at the former SBG companies one by one to see how they have fared in the first years after privatisation.

Taking them in order of sale, **Lowland,** owned by management and employees, quickly dropped the 'Scottish' and set up Lowland Omnibuses Ltd, with a new logo, retaining the green/yellow livery. Lowland operated throughout Borders Region and into Lothian, but with a largely rural and interurban network expansion was not an easy option for Lowland, except at the extremities of its area. In Berwick Lowland and its predecessors had long shared facilities and services with Northumbria and its predecessors, but with Northumbria an unsuccessful bidder for Lowland, the heat has been turned up. Between Haddington and Edinburgh there have been minor skirmishes involving Lowland and SMT, and Lowland has strengthened its East Lothian presence by purchasing Glass of Haddington. Lowland has also gone aggressively into coaching, with some success, which has helped counteract the effects of the recession on Galashiels and Hawick, where once-profitable town services have been affected.

Lowland was the first privatised SBG company to acquire new vehicles – five Scania K113CRB with Plaxton Paramount coach bodies in 1990, and these were followed in 1991 by four Volvo-engined Leyland Tigers with Alexander (Belfast) Q-type bodies, diverted from an Ulsterbus order, and used on long interurban services to Edinburgh. Lowland received Optare Metroriders in 1994, and started a trend towards second-hand Bristol VRTs which has been followed by other former group companies, and is all the more surprising when SBG's notorious 1970s dumping of VRTs on NBC in exchange for Lodekkas is recalled.

Scottish Citylink operated SBG's express service network using liveried coaches, mainly from other

Above:
Kelvin Scottish came into being in 1985, taking over parts of Central, Eastern and Midland. Its original livery was blue and grey, to which a yellow front was later added, as shown on an ex-Midland Fleetline in Kirkintilloch.
STEWART J. BROWN

Below:
There were a number of rethinks on the company's livery during the four-year life of Kelvin Scottish. This distinctive blue and yellow replaced the original grey and blue, but was in turn ousted by a simplified blue/yellow combination. This Olympian came from Eastern Scottish.
STEWART J. BROWN

group fleets, and was sold to its management and employees in August 1990. Set up in the heady early days of express coach deregulation Citylink was now able to shop around for contractors to provide its services and some SBG companies disappeared from Citylink work while less familiar names started to

appear on the legal lettering of Citylink-livered coaches.

The Citylink blue and yellow livery was effectively revamped by Ray Stenning in 1991 and there were further changes to come.

When NBC and SBG were in public ownership

there was close co-operation on cross-border express services, but in the private sector the gloves were off. The situation was further complicated when Stagecoach sold its express services to National Express and Caledonian Express appeared as a new brand-name. After a period of fairly intense competition, Citylink sold out to National Express in 1993, and, whatever the Monopolies and Mergers Commission may decide, peace broke out.

Midland was the first SBG company to go to an outside bidder. GRT Holdings, which had successfully completed the employee buy-out of the Aberdeen municipal fleet, was embarking on the first of its major acquisitions and set about Grampianising the 280-bus Midland fleet, which soon started to appear in an attractive blue/cream version of the Grampian livery, operating as Midland Bluebird with the trademark GRT thistle above the 'i' of Bluebird.

Based at Larbert, with operations throughout Central Region and longer trunk services to Edinburgh and Glasgow, Midland Bluebird Ltd (the company name was changed in 1993) faced limited competition in the Falkirk and Stirling areas, mostly from small minibus operators.

The GRT links have been further emphasised with the transfer of buses and coaches from Aberdeen to Midland, including Leyland Atlanteans which have been used to replace Daimler Fleetlines. New vehicles have been Mercedes-Benz 709s and in 1993-94 0.405s with Wright bodies and similarly-bodied Scania N113s. The isolated Oban area was transferred in 1992 to a new company in which GRT has an interest, Oban & District.

Eastern Scottish went back to the original **SMT** fleetname when it was bought by its management and

employees in 1990. For nearly 60 years from its first operations in 1906 the SMT name had been been familiar, and as many passengers had continued to ignore the Eastern Scottish name adopted in the 1960s the new management sensibly bowed to the undoubted marketing appeal of the old name. A modernised version of the old SMT diamond appeared on the 391 buses operating services throughout Lothian Region and, since deregulation, in Edinburgh.

Eastern had been in competition with its large neighbour, Lothian Region Transport, since October 1986; Eastern had started minibus services in Edinburgh while LRT had expanded beyond the city boundaries into the most lucrative parts of SMT territory. The competition was costly for the privatised SMT, and convenient (and of course totally illegal) 'agreements' of the type reached in other Scottish cities did not appear to be on the table.

SMT has had a tough few years in the private sector, with rumours of its imminent decline ever present. It has survived in spite of aggressive competition from the high-quality LRT operation, and has been able to invest in new vehicles. The first were 30 Renault S56s with Reeve Burgess bodies for its growing minibus operations, in 1991, and the next year 15 Optare Metroriders were allocated to the West

Below:
Midland's Oban operations were sold by GRT to a new company, Oban & District, in which GRT retained a minority interest. This 1981 Leyland Leopard was new to Highland, but had been in the Midland fleet from 1985.
MURDOCH CURRIE

Lothian area. Later in 1993 the first new full-size buses were delivered, 13 Volvo B10B – 12 with Alexander Strider bodies, and one with Wright body. DAF and Dennis Javelin coaches have been taken into the coach fleet.

The future of LRT, still determinedly in public ownership, could affect SMT's longer-term future. The Stagecoach name has been whispered as a likely suitor for either LRT or SMT. In either situation, the future would become very interesting.

One of the most interesting SBG sales was that of 492-bus **Kelvin Central** to its employees. This troubled company, created in the run-up to privatisation, brought together the Kelvin company, operating in and around Glasgow, and the longer-established Central company, with its heartland in Lanarkshire. Neither was in a strong position. Kelvin had suffered in the Glasgow 'bus wars' and Central was still reeling from a seven-week strike early in 1989 that reputedly lost £3 million in revenue and seriously weakened the company's operating base.

Purchasers were not exactly queuing up for KCB and it was a brave act of faith even for the employees to take it on. But they did and set about buying back market share by acquiring smaller companies including, rather surprisingly, Stagecoach's Glasgow-based Magicbus operation. It was suggested at the time that this may not have been unconnected with the Perth company's ambition to buy Strathclyde Buses, but in the event this went to SBL management and employees and a consequence of this has been the closure of KCB's Glasgow operations and a certain

Above:
Strathtay was one of three SBG companies to buy Routemasters as part of its deregulation strategy. They operated in Dundee and, as seen here, Perth. Strathtay later abandoned its Perth operations under pressure from Stagecoach.
STEWART J. BROWN

Left:
For most of the 1970s and the early 1980s Highland used a distinctive poppy red livery with grey and peacock blue relief. This 1979 ECW-bodied Fleetline is still in service, but in a more restrained dark red livery.
STEWART J. BROWN

reallocation of responsibilities in what has now become KCB's heartland.

KCB's mixed inheritance of buses has been further complicated by the vehicles taken over from acquired operators, but in 1993 it received its first new buses, 10 Volvo B10B/Alexanders, similar to the SMT buses, from a Volvo stock order. It is dangerous to make predictions of this kind the best part of a year before

these words will be read, but the prophets of doom and gloom have been proved wrong with KCB, which shows every sign of picking itself up by the bootstraps to recapture some of the prestige its predecessors once enjoyed.

The first sale to Stagecoach was 209-bus **Northern Scottish**, which traded as Bluebird Northern, in 1991. Stagecoach had signalled its intention to bid for all SBG companies but it was known that there were

specific targets; Aberdeen-based Northern, it turned out, was one of them.

An early consequence of the Bluebird purchase was the decision to withdraw from competition on Aberdeen city routes with Grampian, and Grampian's withdrawal from out-of-town services. This has eliminated wasteful competition and Bluebird Buses Ltd (the name adopted in 1992) now faces little competition in its area.

The Stagecoach corporate livery started to replace Northern's yellow-based schemes and soon some of the surfeit of Leyland Olympians were shipped to other group fleets and Bristol VRTs and minibuses were drafted in from other Stagecoach companies.

Bluebird has also benefited from Stagecoach's fleet renewal policies, and has received Mercedes 709s, Dennis Darts, Leyland Olympians and Volvo B10Ms.

The only SBG company to fall into 'foreign' hands has been 164-bus **Strathtay**, which was bought in 1991 by Yorkshire Traction. Outwardly there has been

little change as the fleet retains its blue/orange livery, although there have been fleet additions, courtesy of the parent company. There were some short-lived Bristol VRTs and some minibuses, and new purchases have been two Volvo B10M coaches for Citylink

Above:
Scottish Citylink was the brand name coined for SBG's express coach operations. Initially vehicles were provided by SBG companies, but by the end of the 1980s private-sector contractors were taking a share of the business. This Plaxton-bodied Volvo in Inverness in 1991 belonged to Rapsons.
STEWART J. BROWN

Below:
After privatisation a new Citylink livery was designed by Best Impressions. A Plaxton-bodied B10M of West Coast Motors loads in Oban for Glasgow. After competition between Citylink and National Express, the latter took over the Scottish company in 1993.
STEWART J. BROWN

Above:
Bluebird Northern was the first SBG company to be bought by Stagecoach. A Duple-bodied Tiger in the final version of the pre-Stagecoach livery picks up passengers in Peterhead in 1991, a few months after the Stagecoach takeover.
STEWART J. BROWN

work and five Wright-bodied Dennis Darts.

Aggressive competition from Stagecoach has resulted in a redrawing of the Strathtay boundary. The Perthshire area, including the busy Perth city services, have been surrendered, allowing Strathtay to concentrate on the Dundee and Angus area.

The second Stagecoach purchase in the SBG sell-off was **Fife Scottish** – though not without a fight. Fife management disputed the government's decision to award preferred-bidder status to Stagecoach, but after much legal wrangling this decision was confirmed.

Fife Scottish operates 300 buses throughout the Region of that name, and services in the rural parts of north and east Fife are balanced by those in the densely-populated west Fife.

Competition has been a regular feature of bus services in Fife, most notably in the Glenrothes-Kirkcaldy area where Moffat & Williamson has been a tenacious thorn in Fife's side. Other competitors have come and gone.

The Stagecoach influence quickly made its mark, with vehicle repainting and injections of new buses and coaches. Fife has received Stagecoach-issue buses – Dennis Darts, Volvo B6s and Leyland Olympians – as well as Plaxton Interurban Volvo B10M coaches for

the Stagecoach Express services linking with Edinburgh and Glasgow.

Highland Bus & Coach was sold to a consortium of Clansman and Rapsons in 1991 and has had a chequered career in private ownership. One of the smaller SBG companies, Highland operated urban networks in Inverness and Fort William, and rural and interurban services in a sizeable, though underpopulated, area stretching from Aviemore right to Scotland's northern tip at Thurso and Wick, plus a self-contained island outpost on Skye.

No sooner had Highland emerged into the private sector than Stagecoach mounted an audacious coup.

Facing up to the realities of 1990s bus operation, Highland's new owners were seeking to cut staff wages, which prompted industrial action and gave Stagecoach the opportunity to establish its Inverness Traction subsidiary as the major operator in Inverness. Minibuses were drafted in from other parts of the Stagecoach empire, and Highland drivers were tempted to join the opposition. In a short time the objective had been achieved, and Highland withdrew to concentrate on its operations outside Inverness.

Starting with 141 vehicles, Highland was forced to sell many of its newer vehicles leaving a rump of Leopards, minibuses and an assortment of second-hand double-deckers. When part-owners Citylink sold out to National Express, Rapsons became the owners of Highland and set about salvaging as much as possible of the company.

The last SBG sale, in October 1991, was **Western** which went to its management/employees, but the successful bid was mounted jointly with Clydeside

SBG COMPANIES: WHERE DID THEY GO?

Company	Fleet size			Disposal
	1985	1990	1993	
Central	474	—	—	merged with Kelvin, 1989
Clydeside	334	307	333	merged with Western 1989; purchased from Western by employees aided by Luton & District in 1991
Eastern	367	391	383	management/employees
Fife	300	300	312	Stagecoach
Highland	208	141	120	Clansman/Rapsons, 1991. Rapsons sole owner in 1993
Kelvin	380	492	564	absorbed Central; sold to management/employees
Lowland	104	120	158	management/employees
Midland	292	280	261	GRT Holdings
Northern	254	209	267	Stagecoach
Strathtay	126	164	151	Yorkshire Traction
Western	317	332	346	absorbed Clydeside; sold to management/employees; Clydeside area immediately re-sold (see above)
Scottish Citylink				Clansman Travel (Citylinkmanagement/employees); resold to National Express, 1993

2000, formed to buy the northern part of the area by
previous Clydeside employees and a little help from
Luton & District. This left Western to concentrate on
its Ayrshire/Dumfries & Galloway areas.

Western has retained its black/white/grey/red livery
and traditional style fleetnames, and has quietly got on
with the business of running buses with little or no real
competition to worry about. Its main new vehicle
purchases have been 10 Dennis Darts with Alexander
Dash bodies, diverted from a Stagecoach order, and a
handful of minibuses.

Clydeside 2000, on the other hand, has faced
increasing competition in its Greenock and Paisley
areas from a bewildering host of small minibus
operators, and the company has had to sell newer
buses and close depots to stay afloat. The company

Above:
**Troubles at Highland have seen the sale of modern buses
such as this Olympian, photographed in Inverness in the
summer of 1991, shortly before the company was sold to
Clansman Travel and Rapsons.**
STEWART J. BROWN

has bought large numbers of secondhand Leopards to
compete effectively with low-cost minibuses, and after
a period when the company's future seemed in doubt,
things appear to be more hopeful.

So is there life after Carron House? It is difficult to
avoid the conclusion that privatisation of SBG as a
whole wouldn't have worked. However, some of the
very real fears that were being expressed in 1988 have
turned out to be unfounded.

The threat of the dreaded Stagecoach has for many
employees turned out to be an opportunity: they are
still working for a big company, with as much job
security as the bus industry can offer these days, and
they are getting to drive new vehicles. In general it is
the management/employee-owned companies that face
the most uncertain futures, with a need to repay loans
that makes capital investment difficult.

Has the privatisation been a success? In broad
terms, yes. Many passengers enjoy services at least as
good as they had before, and where they don't it
would be wrong to place the blame at the feet of the
bus operators. Deregulation inevitably means that the

quality of service will vary widely and this is as true in
Scotland as it is elsewhere in Britain. And many of my
former colleagues are still working in the bus industry,
which is important for continuity.

And Carron House? It was built in the late 1960s in
George Street, one of Edinburgh's finest thoroughfares,
and was without doubt one of the ugliest buildings in
the city centre. Scottish Transport Group was its first
occupant, and as the privatisation progressed, STG and
SBG staff gradually abandoned the building until there
was nobody left. Then they pulled it down and replaced
it with a building that matches the Georgian
masterpieces around it.

So while Carron House itself is no more, its legacy
is still alive and well and running buses.

Invasion of the Importers

The last three decades have seen a remarkable change in suppliers of chassis to Britain's bus and coach operators. In 1965 all Britain's buses were British-built. Thirty years on only Dennis survives.
Stewart J. Brown looks back.

It started as a gradual, almost imperceptible movement. Then it became a tidal wave which virtually engulfed British chassis manufacturing. What was it? The rise in sales of imports.

Look way back and you'll find that small numbers of imported chassis have been sold in Britain almost since the dawn of motorbus operation. But by the late 1920s home-based builders large and small had effectively secured the market. And thus it remained right through the war years and into the 1970s.

For most of this time Britain was an exporter of buses — AECs to Australia, Leylands to Latin America. In the colonies there was a ready market, and even after independence most former British colonies continued to buy British bus chassis.

With healthy markets at home and abroad, Britain's bus manufacturing industry just could not fail. It was gradually becoming concentrated in the hands of what grew to be British Leyland, with American-owned Bedford and Ford catering for lower-cost lightweight chassis, generally for coach use.

But just as the sun never sank on the British Empire, it equally never sank on a British-built bus,

toiling away in some far-flung outpost of civilisation.

The first of the modern imports to arrive in the UK was Volvo's B58 coach chassis in 1972. With bus operation concentrated in the hands of public sector companies which had clear pro-British buying policies, Volvo wisely started with a product aimed at private-sector coach operators — the independents as they were known in those far-off days. Unwisely, they had it bodied by Alexander. The Alexander Y-type wasn't really a front-runner when it came to coach body sales — but with the big two, Duple and Plaxton, happily turning out bodies on AEC, Bedford, Ford and Leyland chassis, it is just conceivable that they were none too interested in bodying this Swedish import.

After all, whoever had heard of Volvo, other than as a builder of solid but rather unadventurous cars? In fact, by the following year, both Duple and Plaxton

Below:
As long ago as 1968 Mercedes-Benz was showing interest in the British market with its O.302 integral. But Mercedes coach sales have never taken off — in part at least because of high prices.
ALL UNCREDITED PHOTOGRAPHS BY THE AUTHOR

Above
Scania and MCW targeted major operators with the Metro-Scania, including London Transport which evaluated a batch alongside the Leyland National. The National won.

Below:
Few English operators bought the Ailsa in large numbers. One which did was the West Midlands PTE. Many former West Midlands Ailsas found their way to London when London Buses was trying to reduce its costs in the late 1980s. The Harrow Buses name and livery was used on tendered services in the Harrow area. This Ailsa has Alexander bodywork.

were bodying the B58, conscious that failure to do so could lead to body sales being lost to European builders such as Van Hool, who were already building on Volvo chassis for other markets. So Volvo gradually started rolling in Britain.

Whatever pro-British feelings the public-sector operators had, they were gradually being tempered by the realisation that Leyland was moving towards a monopoly of heavy-duty bus chassis supply. It controlled AEC, Bristol and Daimler. It had eased Guy out of the domestic market, largely because it had no suitable products when the front-engined Arab became obsolescent. Dennis, which had retained its independence, had pulled out of bus production for much the same reasons as Guy — it lacked a suitable modern chassis.

Most large fleets had a fondness for dual-sourcing, but now there were no dual sources. If you bought a double-decker it was coming from BL, whatever the badge on the front might say. And the launch of the standardised Leyland National gave a hint of BL's thinking. Why build three chassis — AEC Swift, Bristol RE and Leyland Panther — to do the same job, when one integral would do it just as well?

It wasn't only the operators who were worried. The bodybuilders were, too. MCW took the bull by the horns and developed its own integral which used Scania units, giving Sweden's other bus builder a way in to the UK bus market. It was a bold move by MCW, pinning their hopes on a high-powered integral with — to UK operators — unknown running units, and it

South Yorkshire PTE's demand for articulated buses could not be met by British manufacturers. MAN supplied five from Germany, which ran in Sheffield alongside Anglo-Danish Leyland DABs. A MAN is seen on trial in London.

paid off moderately well. The fact that Metro-Scania production totalled only 133 had as much to do with a change in operating policies by MCW's customers as with any failings in their new Anglo-Swedish product.

That the Metro-Scania had a remarkable thirst for diesel at a time when the words 'fuel crisis' were on everyone's lips didn't help — but it really was a victim of the rapid return from urban single-deck to double-deck operation following the legalisation of

Below:
Coach deregulation opened up opportunities for Neoplan with its high-capacity three-axle Skyliner. One loads in Glasgow in 1983, when Stagecoach was a relatively small-scale operator of express services.

double-deckers which were one-man-operated.

MCW responded to the changing trend with a double-deck version of its Scania-powered bus, the Metropolitan. This did significantly better — over 660 were built — but was arguably one of the great follies of modern bus engineering. It was very thirsty and the steel-framed body suffered severe corrosion. The latter problem forced most Metropolitan operators to abandon the type when they were due for compulsory recertification at seven years. The fuel companies no doubt regretted their passing rather more than the operators.

Fleet operators who bought Metropolitans included Hull, Leicester, London Transport, Newport and the PTEs at Greater Glasgow, Merseyside, South Yorkshire and Tyne & Wear. But after five years MCW and Scania went their separate ways with Scania supplying chassis and MCW developing a new Gardner-powered integral, the Metrobus.

Meanwhile the other Swedish manufacturer was looking at buses too. Volvo's contribution to the single-deck bus market was a solitary rear-engined B59 demonstrator with Marshall body. It remained unique. No other B59s were sold in Britain.

Volvo's importer was Ailsa Trucks, based in Scotland, and this had two immediate effects. Firstly, Volvo coaches sold disproportionately well to Scottish coach operators who abandoned their Reliances and Leopards for this new and more powerful Swedish chassis with good local service support. Parks of Hamilton were among the early users of the B58 and after buying them bought few chassis from British builders.

Secondly, it led to the birth of the Ailsa. Designed to pander to the Scottish Bus Group's dislike of troublesome rear-engined chassis, the Ailsa was developed and built in Scotland by Ailsa Trucks using Volvo's turbocharged 6.7-litre truck engine in a perimeter frame chassis. The engine was compact and relatively light, overcoming the weight problems of the hefty Gardner unit used in the Guy Wulfrunian of similar layout 15 years earlier.

The front engine was noisy, but it also released enough space at the rear of the lower saloon for another row of seats. A mid-1970s Ailsa typically seated 79, compared with 74 on a Fleetline or Atlantean.

Volvo took over the Ailsa Trucks operation and with it the Ailsa. It remained something of a specialist beast, but sold in respectable quantities for the best part of a decade, and not just to the Scottish Bus Group whose conservatism had spawned it. The Greater Glasgow PTE built up a large fleet, which broke Leyland's virtual monopoly in Scotland's biggest bus operation. Tayside, too, standardised on the Ailsa after a disastrous affair with the Bristol VRT. In England, the South Yorkshire PTE was the biggest user, but smaller numbers were run by Derby and Merseyside. In Wales, Cardiff City Transport took two sizeable batches.

The Ailsa wasn't a bad bus. But apart from operators like SBG, most fleets were accepting, as well they might after 15 years, that the back of a bus was the best place for an engine to be. It insulated passengers and the driver from noise. And it was accessible for maintenance — even if it did need more of it than the trusty old front-engined half-cab 'deckers that were still a common sight on city streets.

The Ailsa also helped Volvo sell 716 buses in the UK (plus over 300 abroad) which it otherwise wouldn't have sold.

So, by the mid-1970s the two Swedish builders had gained a toehold in the market. Volvo was selling small — but increasing — numbers of coaches and the Ailsa double-decker. Scania was supplying running units to MCW, and thus gaining an entry to some of MCW's prestigious big city fleet customers.

Mercedes-Benz, one of the giants of the European automotive industry, was also taking an interest — but not very successfully. It had actually exhibited an O.302 integral coach at Earls Court in 1968. Then it showed a Plaxton-bodied underframe. But what it didn't show was commitment and its coach sales didn't take off. Indeed, they have not taken off even now, despite further forays into the market with Jonckheere, Plaxton and small numbers of O.303 integrals.

With buses Mercedes fared no better. Two Northern Counties-bodied O.305s for the Selnec PTE appeared in 1973. But they were not the precursors of a great German invasion. The Germans had to wait for a revolution before they could safely invade. That came in 1985 with the arrival of minibuses.

Back to the 1970s. A few continental builders were showing some slight interest in Britain, the most successful of which was UTIC from Portugal, selling integral coaches on the strength of their AEC running units.

But one more major player was to arrive on the

scene. Best known as builders of funny little cars which were allegedly powered by rubber bands, DAF's first coach for a British operator appeared in 1975. They repeated the pattern set by Volvo, with steady annual increases in sales — until 1982 and a fleet deal with Shearings, DAF's first big order in the UK, found the Dutch manufacturer's product and service support wanting and this hit sales growth hard.

DAF's first UK offering was the mid-engined MB which used a horizontal 11.6-litre engine whose parentage could be traced back to Leyland's O.600. This was followed by the rear-engined SB, powered by a smaller vertical 8.25-litre unit.

At the end of the 1970s BL's coach range was, to put not too fine a point on it, outdated. The AEC Reliance, popular among independents, was axed in 1979. The Leyland Leopard was achieving high sales, but that was only because it was the standard choice for SBG and National Bus Company subsidiaries whose coaching operations generally suffered from the dead hand of the big company ethos. The Leopard was replaced by the much-improved Tiger in 1981.

But by this time Volvo coach sales were shooting ahead, virtually doubling each year from 1977, when 50 were sold, to 1980 when sales peaked at 393. However, it was not until 1986 that sales of the B10M (the B58's successor) overtook sales of Leyland's Leopard/Tiger models. Leyland's sales figures were always boosted by Leopard and Tiger buses for Ulsterbus and the Scottish Bus Group; in reality Volvo coaches were outselling Leylands by the early 1980s.

But Volvo and DAF were not the only contenders for British coach operators' custom. From 1979 a number of new players appeared. MAN introduced its SR280 integral and managed to sell a couple of dozen a year in the early 1980s. Another German builder, Setra, joined the fray with its expensive but high-quality coaches.

Opposite page:
Scania's first foray into the British bus business in the late 1960s was a joint venture with MCW, the Metro-Scania. Customers included Leicester City Transport.

Top left:
Volvo was the first importer to make a significant impact on British coaching. An early customer was Park's of Hamilton. This Plaxton-bodied B58 is seen when new in 1973. Park's livery at the time was unrelieved black.

Centre left:
Scottish-based Ailsa Trucks developed the Volvo-powered Ailsa for the Scottish Bus Group. All of the early Ailsas had Alexander bodies, as illustrated by this Alexander (Fife) example in Kirkcaldy.

Left:
Volvo adapted its best-selling B10M chassis to produce the Citybus, the first successful underfloor-engined double-decker in Britain. The prototype, with Marshall body, entered service with the Greater Glasgow PTE in 1982.

Top:
LAG initially offered bodies on chassis, before launching the Panoramic integral as shown here running for Titterington of Penrith. LAG was later taken over by Van Hool.

Above
The SB220 established DAF in the city bus market, initially in partnership with Optare who developed the attractive Delta body. This is a Northumbria SB220 in central Newcastle.

MAN had earlier hit the headlines when it supplied five articulated buses to the South Yorkshire PTE for operation in Sheffield. SYPTE's interest in artics saw Leyland import two batches of DAB articulated buses from its Danish subsidiary. The first were bodied at the Leyland National factory in Workington; the second delivery were complete DAB vehicles. Workington-bodied DABs were also supplied to British Airways. Mercedes-Benz and Volvo also showed an interest in artics, bringing over left-hand-drive demonstrators. Volvo was going to supply a right-hand-drive chassis to be bodied as a coach by Duple. However, the government passed legislation which banned articulated coaches from the outside

lane of motorways. This killed any interest in artic coaches amongst British express service operators.

The deregulation of coach services in 1980 opened up an opportunity for Neoplan, whose high-capacity Skyliner double-deck quickly became a familiar sight on British motorways. Neoplan also sold smaller numbers of single-deckers, including some which shared the Skyliner's three-axle layout.

It was a Dutch builder, Bova, which popularised the rear-engined integral coach with the low-priced DAF-powered Europa in 1981. It was followed by the Futura in 1983 and was joined briefly by the Calypso, which was the marriage of a Duple body and a Bova underframe. A number of coach manufacturers anticipated that British operators would move away from body-on-chassis coaches to continental style rear-engined integrals and this saw companies such as Van Hool and LAG offer complete coaches in the UK. But the big switch to integrals never happened, as

Above
Setra has an enviable reputation for the production of high-quality coaches. A Bebb coach pauses at the bus station in Heathrow Airport while on National Express service in 1991.

Below:
Yorkshire Rider is one of the biggest users of Scania's N113. A batch of 35 with Alexander Strider bodies entered service in 1993.

British buyers remained stubbornly loyal to proven mid-engined chassis from Volvo and Leyland.

Scania — who had demonstrated a 260bhp integral coach to the National Bus Company as early as 1973 — moved into the coach business in 1982 with the rear-engined K112 underframe. It was soon selling 50 a year. Scania turned its attention to buses too and with its N112 rear-engined underframe was able to cater for operators requiring either single- or double-deckers. At first only Newport bought N-series single-deckers, but by the end of the 1980s they were appearing in a number of fleets.

Sales of Scania double-deckers started slowly, seldom exceeding single figures each year in the early and mid-1980s, but towards the end of the decade and into the 1990s a small number of significant fleet orders boosted Scania's sales. Notable Scania double-deck users included London Buses, Busways, West Midlands Travel and Yorkshire Rider.

The K112 and the later K113 and smaller-engined K92/K93 featured an in-line rear engine. The K92 and K93 were used by a number of operators as the base for a single-deck bus and by one — Maidstone Boro'line — for a pair of 92-seat double-deckers in 1987. The K112/K113 were also bodied as three-axle double-deck coaches.

Meanwhile Volvo was re-appraising its strategy. Ailsa deliveries had peaked at just under 150 as early as 1976. Thereafter they had averaged around 80 a

UK CHASSIS AND INTEGRAL IMPORTERS: 1994

Company	Manufacturing bases
Blue Bird	USA
Bova	Holland
DAF Bus	Holland
Iveco	Italy
MAN	Germany
Mercedes-Benz	Germany
Neoplan	Germany
Scania	Sweden
Setra	Germany/Spain
Van Hool	Belgium
Volvo	Sweden/Scotland

...and those who've come and gone

DAB	Denmark
FAP FAMOS (a)	Yugoslavia
GAC	Ireland
LAG (b)	Belgium
Magirus Deutz (c)	Germany
Renault	France/England
UTIC	Portugal
TAZ	Yugoslavia

(a) marketed as Ensign Charisma
(b) now taken over by Van Hool
(c) now part of Iveco

Above:
Renault made an attempt to sell big buses in Britain with its PR100, bodied in Wigan by Northern Counties. The original demonstrator is seen in service with Southampton Citybus.

year and by the middle of the 1980s had fallen to under 50. The front-engined layout worked, but it wasn't ideal and so was born the Citybus, based on the

Above:
Scanias have found considerable popularity among small coach operators. Perry's of Slingsby, in North Yorkshire, run this K93 with Plaxton Premiere body.

mid-engined B10M coach chassis.

The first was bodied by Marshall for the Greater Glasgow PTE, whose successor, Strathclyde Buses, became the biggest user of the type, building up a fleet of 101. The Citybus appeared in 1982 and, like the Ailsa which it replaced, offered higher seating capacity than its rear-engined competitors. But, again like the Ailsa, it proved to be something of a specialist taste. Sizeable numbers were bought by London Buses and Grey-Green, while other significant users included Nottingham, Derby and Northampton — by 1993 the last-named was the only Citybus buyer and the model's long-term future looked less than secure.

By this time, of course, Volvo had taken over Leyland Bus and was producing an updated Olympian at its Irvine truck and bus factory, alongside its B6 midibus chassis. It no longer needed the Citybus to maintain its presence in the market for double-deck buses.

And what of the others? Mercedes-Benz finally succeeded in the British bus market with the move to minibuses and by the start of the 1990s was out-selling all other minibus makers. On the back of this success it tackled the big bus market, offering its O.405 range with bodywork by Alexander and Wright. The only fleet orders so far have come from GRT Holdings for two of its Scottish companies, Grampian Transport and Midland Bluebird.

The buoyant minibus market in the mid-1980s attracted Renault and Iveco. The French manufacturer offered Dunstable-built models and then pulled out of the bus business in Britain when the decision was made to cease building trucks at Dunstable. The last British Renaults entered service at the start of 1993.

The company also had a brief flirtation with full-sized buses, linking up with Northern Counties in 1988 to sell the ageing PR100 rear-engined model which dated back to the early 1970s. Renault supplied PR100 chassis and Northern Counties built French-style bodies. Only five were produced. There had also been plans at Renault to sell the award-winning FR1 integral coach, but these got no further than the exhibition of a left-hand-drive demonstrator at coach rallies in 1985 and 1990.

Iveco's small bus was the Italian-built Fiat 49.10,

Above:
Iveco's success has been with small buses. This is an Italian-built 59.12 with unusual two-door Mellor bodywork running in Oxford for Thames Transit.

and this was followed by similar, bigger, models. Ivecos could be found in a number of fleets, including London Buses, in the heady days of the mid-1980s. But in the 1990s most bus operators were buying Mercs, and Transit Holdings was the only major user of Ivecos for bus work.

Iveco, like Mercedes, has tried to move into bigger buses. A handful of rear-engined 315 midi-coaches were sold, most with French-built bodies by Lorraine (an Iveco-owned company which was bought by Plaxton in 1988). A front-engined midibus, the truck-based 70.14, was a flop in 1989. Then came the TurboCity 100 double-decker in 1991 which looks set to be an even bigger flop. One demonstrator was bodied by Alexander. The TurboCity 100 suffers from being a single-deck design with a long rear overhang which creates difficulties with weight on the rear axle. This in turn compromised the seating layout at the rear

Below:
US manufacturer Blue Bird started supplying coaches to Britain in a small way in 1993. The styling may be dated, but the low price could attract some buyers.

of the bus.

The TurboCity 100 was followed by the TurboCity 50, a single-decker based on the same chassis. Alexander once again bodied a demonstrator (in 1992), and this was followed by another with WS Vanguard body in 1993. Whether there is room for Iveco in the highly-competitive UK bus market is open to question.

MAN disappeared from the scene in the early 1980s, but re-appeared later in the decade with a small rear-engined coach chassis bodied by Caetano and Berkhof. Then came a link with Optare, which saw the MAN 11.190 chassis being used as the basis of the Optare Vecta, a single-decker introduced in 1991. MAN has also been selling small numbers of 12m coach chassis in the 1990s and plans to expand its UK coach business.

MAN's Optare link followed the success of Optare's CityPacer minibus, based on a MAN-VW LT55 chassis and introduced in 1986. The eye-catching CityPacer was bought by London Buses and Blackpool Transport, but most were sold to small operators and sales dropped dramatically after Optare took over production of the MetroRider minibus from MCW in 1989.

Other continental builders thought deregulated Britain might open up bus sales opportunities. Van Hool and Neoplan both brought demonstrators into the country in 1988-89 with Neoplan even contemplating local assembly by its importer, Carlton PSV. More recently Neoplan has benefited from growing interest in ultra-low-floor buses and a fleet of 11 Neoplan N4014s is running in Merseyside.

DAF has continued to sell coaches in quite respectable numbers and moved into the bus business in 1988 with its rear-engined SB220 underframe. Initially this was available only with Optare Delta bodywork and the DAF/Optare combination set new design standards for urban buses in Britain. The SB220 was from 1990 also available with Hungarian-

built Ikarus bodywork, the first example of Eastern bloc bus bodywork in Britain.

The Eastern bloc was making its presence felt in the coach market with two integrals being offered in Britain in 1989 — the TAZ Dubrava, marketed by Midlands-based dealer DSB, and the Ensign Charisma, sold by Ensign Bus of Essex. Both had Mercedes engines and came from Yugoslavia — and both were short-lived even without the problems caused by Yugoslavia's vicious civil war.

DAF and Optare also collaborated on a double-decker, the DAF DB250 which was unveiled in 1991. This was marketed as the Optare Spectra and did for double-deck styling what the Delta had done for single-deckers. However, it did not have the same instant sales success; the only large fleet order so far has come from London Buses. By this time DAF Bus and Optare were part of United Bus which collapsed in the autumn of 1993. Both DAF Bus and Optare survived the collapse under new independent ownership.

Turn the clock back 20 years and in 1975 you will find importers playing a very small part in the British bus and coach business. In total 4,900 new vehicles were put into service of which almost 3,100 were from the British Leyland stable. The only importers were Volvo (123 B58 coaches) and Mercedes-Benz with a solitary O.302. There were also 24 Volvo-powered but British-built Ailsas, and just under 200 Scania-inspired MCW Metropolitans.

Now the situation is rather different. In 1993, a total of 2,300 new buses and coaches entered service. The only British-owned manufacturer is Dennis. The only other heavy-duty British-built chassis are Volvo's Olympian and B6. Volvo's dominance of the market means that almost 50% of big bus and coach chassis are still British-built, even if many come from a Swedish-owned factory. Volvo's B10M and B10B single-deckers are built in Sweden.

Scania remains active, even if its sales lag well behind Volvo's. DAF's position has been weakened by the company's failure in 1993 which looks set to affect sales of buses more than of coaches, not least because of Optare's search for new chassis partners. Mercedes' strength remains with minibuses, as does Iveco's. Renault has come and gone.

American builder Blue Bird is making a pitch for sales with a range which does not seem particularly well-suited to British operations. Trans-Atlantic automotive styling flair seems to stop with cars and trucks; the Blue Bird has a distinctly old-fashioned air. And where next? Who dare forecast? All of the major European chassis manufacturers are agreed on one thing — by the end of the century they will not all still be in business in their present form. Renault and Volvo nearly amalgamated at the start of 1994 — then Volvo called the deal off at the last minute. It would be a braver man than I who would try to forecast the survivors — and which of them will be selling buses in Britain in the year 2000.

Below:
Volvo is now Britain's major supplier of buses and coaches from factories in Sweden and Scotland. The first Swedish-built rear-engined B10Bs entered service in 1993 as successors to the Leyland Lynx. Northern Counties bodied this example for Liverbus.

Above:
Accrington. This charming view dates from 1959. The crew of an East Lancs-bodied Guy Arab give directions to a passing motorist in an Austin A40 van. Accrington's buses were painted in a distinctive dark blue, black and red. In 1974 the operation passed to the newly-created Hyndburn authority.   ALL PHOTOGRAPHS BY THE AUTHOR

Municipal Miscellany

Lancashire in the 1950s boasted no fewer than 29 municipal bus operators. **Roy Marshall** illustrates some of the variety to be found among those fleets outside the big urban areas, the fleets which survived the formation of the PTEs.

The Lancashire municipals

There were 29 municipal bus fleets serving Lancashire 40 years ago and between them they ran almost 5,500 buses. They were:

Accrington	
Ashton-under-Lyne	Oldham
Barrow-in-Furness	Preston
Blackburn	Ramsbottom
Blackpool	Rawtenstall
Bolton	Rochdale
Burnley, Colne & Nelson	St Helens
Bury	Salford
Darwen	Southport
Haslingden	Stalybridge, Hyde,
Lancaster	Mossley &
Leigh	Dukinfield
Liverpool	Stockport
Lytham St Annes	Warrington
Manchester	Widnes
Morecambe & Heysham	Wigan

The first to go was Haslingden, joined with Rawtenstall in 1968 in the new Rossendale undertaking. The creation of the Passenger Transport Executives in 1969 saw the disappearance of 12. A further eight went when local government was reorganised in 1974 — three being absorbed by the expansion of the PTE operating areas, two disappearing into the fleets of larger neighbours, and three being taken into other counties as Lancashire's boundaries were redrawn.

So 20 years ago the number in Lancashire had dropped to eight — Blackburn, Blackpool, Burnley & Pendle, Fylde, Hyndburn, Lancaster, Preston and Rossendale. Since 1993 the number has fallen further, as local authorities have sold their bus operations under pressure from central government. Fylde, Lancaster and Preston no longer have local authority-owned bus operations, bringing the number of survivors of Lancashire's great days of municipal bus operation down to five — and even their future in public ownership cannot be considered secure.

Above:

Barrow-in-Furness. The unkind joke about Barrow is that it lies at the end of England's longest cul-de-sac. In 1959, when this photograph was taken, that cul-de-sac was firmly in Lancashire. The redrawing of boundaries in 1974 moved it to Cumbria. The bus is a 1949 Leyland Titan PD2 which had been newly rebodied by Roe. Its original wooden-framed Park Royal body had proved unsound. Although Barrow moved out of Lancashire in 1974, its municipal bus operation continued until 1989 when the pressures of deregulation forced its closure. Ribble took over some of its services.

Below:

Blackburn. Guy's postwar success was built on buses such as this 1945 Arab with Massey bodywork, seen in Blackburn bus station in 1952. Indeed Blackburn was one of a number of municipal operators to buy substantial numbers of Guys after World War 2 and a postwar Arab III is visible in the background. Note the municipal crest on both decks and the complex lining-out. The town's bus station is still on the same site, but now offers somewhat improved facilities.

Above:
Blackpool. Fully-fronted buses were introduced to the town in the 1930s and were still being bought in the 1950s even if the later examples were rather less exuberant than their prewar and early postwar counterparts. This is Lytham terminus in 1959 with the driver taking a break alongside a fine bus shelter. The Kings Road Garage was selling Standard Triumph cars — now, like this Metro-Cammell-bodied PD2, no more than a memory.

Below:
Burnley, Colne & Nelson. Single-deckers were relatively uncommon in the Lancashire municipal fleets, but BC&N always had a number for routes which were unsuitable for double-deckers or carried small numbers of passengers. This 1950 Massey-bodied Leyland Tiger PS1 is seen in Burnley centre in 1958. By this time some single-deckers had been converted for driver-only operation — but not this one which still needed a conductor because of its rear entrance. The BC&N operation became Burnley & Pendle in 1974.

Above:
Darwen. Darwen was one of the smaller fleets and one of its Crossleys is seen in Blackburn bus station in 1951 waiting to take up a journey south to Darwen Cemetery. The Darwen fleet, like that of its larger neighbour, did not carry exterior advertising. Darwen was absorbed by an enlarged Blackburn operation in 1974 and for a time the new fleet livery incorporated both town's colours — red for Darwen and green for Blackburn.

Below:
Haslingden. This Leyland Titan PD1 was Haslingden's first postwar bus and had an Alexander body built to Leyland designs. The Haslingden fleet disappeared in 1968, being merged with neighbouring Rawtenstall.

Above:
Lancaster. The ignominious end of municipal bus operation in Lancaster was still over 40 years off when this 1940 Daimler COG5 with Willowbrook body was photographed in the city's bus station in 1952. Cephos appeared to offer a cure for a multitude of ailments. Lancaster City Transport ceased running in 1993, leaving the city's bus services to Ribble.

Below:
Lytham St Annes. Lytham St Annes, genteel neighbour to brash Blackpool, ran in a dignified blue and off-white livery. Inspired no doubt by its bigger neighbour, it bought full-fronted buses in the late 1930s, including this Leyland-bodied Titan seen in St Annes in 1952. These buses were long-lived, some giving the town 25 years of service. Lytham St Annes' buses passed to Fylde Borough Council in 1974 and the operation was privatised at the end of 1993.

Above:
Rawtenstall. Just as Leyland was the major chassis supplier to most Lancashire municipals, Blackburn-based East Lancashire Coachbuilders had a loyal following as a body supplier, particularly to the smaller fleets. This East Lancs-bodied PD2 was new in 1948 and was unusual in having a four-bay body; most East Lancs bodies were of five-bay construction. Rawtenstall became Rossendale in 1968.

Opposite top:
Morecambe & Heysham. This smart Park Royal-bodied AEC Regent III — a relatively unusual choice in Leyland's heartland — was four years old when photographed in 1952. Many of M&H's buses enjoyed long operational lives and this one was later preserved. When local authority boundaries were changed in 1974 the M&H bus fleet was absorbed by neighbouring Lancaster.

Opposite bottom:
Preston. Only six miles from Leyland, it is no surprise that Preston was a loyal Leyland user. This PD2 with Leyland's Farington-style body is seen when new in 1954. It was rebuilt as a 30ft-long PD3 in 1963. The livery was maroon and light cream. Until 1980 Preston used route letters rather than numbers. The Preston bus operation was sold to its managers and employees in 1993.

Top:
Warrington. Since 1974 in Cheshire, Warrington was part of Lancashire when this photograph was taken in 1956. Both buses are unusual in municipal service — a Bristol K6G on the left and a Foden PVD6 on the right. The Foden has an East Lancs body while the Bristol was bodied by Bruce.

Above:
Widnes. Also moved to Cheshire in 1974 (and renamed Halton at the same time), Widnes operated this wartime Daimler, a Massey-bodied CWA6. It is seen in 1950 in a part of the town which is still recognisable the best part of half a century later — even if the buses have changed beyond recognition. The fleet's 1990s single-deckers can carry more passengers than this 1940s double-decker.

Seeing RED in BATH

Red interlopers from London added some colour to Bath's streets in 1992-93.
Martin Curtis tells the tale.

London buses which have worked in Bath on loan to Badgerline between October 1992 and March 1994.

Altogether, six vehicles were involved, although the first was not really a London bus at all but was, nevertheless, finished in London Buses red and grey colours. This was a Plaxton Verde demonstrator (J120

Below:
The red-liveried Dennis Lance demonstrator on service 14B outside Bath Spa station.
ALL PHOTOGRAPHS BY THE AUTHOR

The City of Bath, with its Georgian architecture and rich history dating back to Roman times – and beyond – is dominated in transport terms by the InterCity Great Western line from Paddington (which is elevated through the city centre) and by the Badgerline buses which provide an intensive network of local services.

Since the division of the former Bristol Omnibus Co, Badgerline's green and yellow liveries have become an accepted and essential part of the Bath scene with an operation involving both minibuses and full-size vehicles, which maintain both city and inter-urban services. A highly successful open-top tour is also provided in partnership with Guide Friday – which has attracted two rival 'copy cat' operations from local independent concerns. Up to 170 vehicles can be based at Badgerline's Bath (Kensington) Depot – which is the largest in the entire Badgerline group.

However, the dominance of Badgerline's fleet was diluted, just a little, by a succession of red-liveried

SPF) based on a Dennis Lance chassis which was among several single-deckers to be evaluated by Badgerline, and which resulted in a substantial order for similar vehicles which have enabled companies in the Badgerline Group to update their single-deck fleets.

Having previously operated for a trial period from Badgerline's Bristol (Marlborough Street) Depot, the Plaxton-bodied Lance was allocated to route 14 upon its arrival in Bath (running from Odd Down to Weston village via the city centre) which was normally the domain of Bristol VRTs and Leyland Nationals.

Before the Lance's departure on 12 October 1992, a second single-deck Dennis had arrived in Bath for demonstration, this time Wright-bodied Dart DW115 (LDZ9115) from London Buses CentreWest. While this bus was rather shorter than most single-deckers, it too was allocated to the 14s and, while painted in identical colours to the Lance, attracted an astonishing amount of passenger comment simply because it

Above:
London Buses' Wright-bodied Dart DW115 about to commence its first revenue-earning journey for Badgerline in Dorchester Street, Bath. It carries the Badgerline fleetname in the nearside windscreen.

retained London Buses and Gold Arrow lettering. Passengers and staff were invited to comment on both Lance and Dart, and it was surprising how much the London identity on the Dart attracted additional attention. Not least among the reactions this generated was surprise from passengers emerging from Bath Spa railway station who had disembarked from a London train, and momentarily wondered if they had stepped off at the wrong station! – having noticed identical vehicles at the beginning of their journey around Paddington.

An order for Dennis Darts also followed from Badgerline and while the bodywork by Wrights was impressive, the Badgerline vehicles have Plaxton Pointer coachwork.

Bath's next encounter with a London bus occurred a few months later, in April 1993. This involved the highly successful open-top tour operation – which had become so successful that Badgerline had doubled its fleet on tour work (with 11 open-top or convertible vehicles in tour livery including a 1941 Bristol K5G normally used on Saturdays) and trebled its passenger loadings.

In addition, rival operators had appeared and the City Council, encouraged by several residents' groups but especially those in Royal Crescent, had been seeking ways to limit the tour operations. The matter was passed to Avon County Council as highway authority which, having already banned coaches from Royal Crescent, had effectively forced more

passengers on to the tour buses.

Despite a range of voluntary restrictions already imposed by the operators, a proposal was put forward to restrict tour buses by a form of licensing – but this in turn provoked considerable controversy as the tour buses, with their hop-on, hop-off facility, had become the main method of travel for many tourists – on whom the city relies so heavily.

Hoteliers and the local Chamber of Commerce were among those to enter the debate by opposing bus restrictions while nationally the Bus & Coach Council

Below:
London Pride's enormous MCW Metroliner turns from Terrace Walk while operating on 'The Bath Tour'.

also became involved since the method of licensing proposed appeared to be completely contrary to the 1985 Transport Act with its emphasis on deregulation.

Several years of lengthy negotiations had already resulted in operators compromising and restraining aspects of their services (including commentary restrictions) but some were still not satisfied and the debate raged. At a meeting of the County Council's Planning, Highways and Transport Committee during February 1993, a decision to pursue formal restrictions was passed by one vote. It had been pointed out that such proposed restrictions would fail to meet demand, conjuring-up images of Bath's visitors being divided into those selected to view Royal Crescent and those refused. The opportunity was therefore taken to bring a much larger open-top bus to Bath (most of Badgerline's tour buses being open-top Bristol VRT/SLs) as a means of carrying more if restrictions were to be based on numbers of vehicles, and London Pride obliged by producing one of their enormous six-wheel Metroliners, with seating for over 60 on the top deck alone!

Many Badgerline staff saw this type of vehicle for the first time when, on a Sunday in March 1993, a Badgerline double-decker full of Bath Tour drivers and guides (including Guide Friday staff with whom Badgerline jointly operate the Bath Tour) made the reverse trip to the capital to view London tours, and critically compare their operation with those in London.

The London Pride Metroliner (377, B117 ORU) was used on one journey only on Monday, 5 April 1993 but attracted press, local TV and radio coverage and appeared to have a profound influence on the open-top debate in Bath. Within days, Avon County Councillors had reversed their decision to introduce licensing in favour of maintaining voluntary restrictions!

Later, during May 1993 it was again possible to ride on a London bus in Bath. And not just a London bus – but arguably the ultimate London bus design, the Routemaster. And not just one – but two! This came about through discussions between members of Badgerline and London Buses' CentreWest managements. London Buses had a requirement to place these vehicles in Bath for a series of special hires and arrangements were made to garage them at Badgerline's Kensington Depot, but between their commitments for hires they would be loaned to Badgerline for use on 'The Bath Tour' – complete with Guide Friday guides. This offered a unique opportunity for trials with yet another type of vehicle – and of a design not previously seen in regular service in the West of England.

The vehicles in question were both refurbished Routemasters with Cummins engines, the first: RMC1510 (510 CLT) an ex-Green Line coach which was suitably converted to open-top, while the second was RML2735 (SMK 735F) a conventional covered-top bus.

On Saturday, 22 May 1993 both worked on 'The Bath Tour'. Most popular of the two was the RMC as good weather made the RML a less attractive proposition. But heads certainly turned at the sight of these buses in Bath – and a little confusion resulted, with some passengers having to be coaxed on to red Routemaster buses clutching their Badgerline/Guide Friday tickets as the main rival operator of open-top buses also runs red (almost maroon) buses, including London DMSs.

The Routemasters were not available for Badgerline use on Sunday, 23 May and the RML had to return to London to take up normal duties in time for Monday morning rush-hour, but the RMC stayed on until 1 June, and was used regularly between private hires.

Above:
RML2735 creeps along the cobbles of Bath's Royal Crescent, whose residents would prefer to see no buses and fewer tourists.

Their operation produced some extremely interesting information. Their new engines produced ample power on the steep gradients out of the city which forms part of Badgerline's tour (and are not attempted by the city's rival tour operators). The sight of red Routemasters in Bath's Royal Crescent was also not appreciated by some residents – who among other things objected to their colour (but nor was a small green Mercedes-Benz minibus operated the same week as an experiment linked to the city's environment week, in an attempt to reduce visual impact). The problem in this area is that some residents appear simply to object to visiting tourists per se!

Many passengers rode on the RMs because they were 'proper' London buses and different from Badgerline's usual vehicles, but others avoided them, preferring instead the appearance and reassurance of Badgerline's own primrose and green Bristol VRs on

Above
The RMC and RML side by side at Terrace Walk while running together on 'The Bath Tour'.

which award-winning high standards have been achieved for tourists. Many of the drivers in Bath certainly liked the RMs, however, and considerable rivalry existed to be allocated one.

The sixth London bus was received in Bath direct from the manufacturers on 10 February 1994 and remained until 9 March 1994, during which time it operated on city service 5 connecting Whiteway and Twerton with the city centre. Potentially this bus was to have a greater influence on bus design and subsequent orders than any of the other London vehicles used, for it was a Dennis Super Low Floor SLF Lance with Wright coachwork, wearing Uxbridge Buses fleetname and number LLW17. The benefits of such an accessible vehicle to not only the elderly and disabled but also the able-bodied and particularly young mothers with prams and pushchairs was remarkable — and whilst not certain, could yet lead the way forward for future bus design, including minibus and double-deck applications incorporating this level of accessibility. Investigations immediately followed to explore whether funding and infrastructure changes could allow a whole route in Bath to become operated by low-floor vehicles.

If nothing else, the London bus interludes added interest briefly to the

Bath scene – and more importantly have made contributions by offering first-hand experience of several types of unfamiliar designs. Currently, there are no further plans for visits to Bath by London buses – but in view of what has operated there in the 18 months from October 1992, who can be sure of what might appear in future!

Below:
High above Bath's city centre in wintry conditions, Uxbridge Buses' Dennis Lance SLF climbs towards Whiteway Circle

False **Dawn**

Urban single-deckers have become
increasingly popular in the 1990s —
but not for the first time, as
John Burnett demonstrates with a
look at some of those in the north.

F ew would argue that there is a distinct move
towards rear-engined single-deckers as the standard
configuration for British service buses. But whether or
not double-deckers will be totally eclipsed is another
matter.

Thirty years ago there appeared to be a similar

Below:
**The first production AEC Swift chassis, number MP2R001,
was bodied by Willowbrook and used as a
demonstrator. It is seen in the demonstration park
outside Glasgow's Kelvin Hall during the 1965 Scottish
Motor Show.** ALL PHOTOGRAPHS BY THE AUTHOR

process taking place. The law prevented one-man-
operation of double-deckers and the trades unions
were also opposed to the idea. Many of the double-
deckers being withdrawn at that time could seat only
53 or 56 and their replacement by 11m-long saloons of
broadly similar capacity seemed like a good idea.

The major manufacturers of the time — Leyland,
AEC, Daimler and Bristol — produced new models
with rear engines allowing much easier entrance and
exit arrangements than had been possible on the 1950s
generation of underfloor-engined single-deckers.

However, there was a snag. Apart from the Bristol
RE, which was initially available only to state-owned
operators, the others seemed either not to work very
well (Leyland Panther and Panther Cub, AEC Swift
and Merlin) or hardly at all (Daimler Roadliner).

Daimler then produced a single-deck version of the
successful Fleetline chassis which enjoyed slightly
better sales success than the Roadliner and a very
much longer average life span.

The relative lack of success of these models may
have taught the manufacturing industry an important
lesson: the Leyland National which followed was
subjected to a most rigorous design and development
programme before being launched on to the market.

Above:
In 1965 Stockton Corporation purchased a pair of Leyland Panther Cubs with dual-door Park Royal bodywork. Two more followed in 1966. None lasted more than 10 years.

Below:
This Sunderland Corporation Daimler Roadliner lasted only five years in service, being withdrawn in 1971 and then used as a source of spare parts to keep two identical sister vehicles on the road. They ran only for a further three years before their owner — by this time the Tyne & Wear PTE — gave up the unequal struggle. The distinctive bodywork was built by Strachans to Sunderland's designs.

Above:
Darlington Corporation's first one-man buses were Roe-bodied Cummins-engined Daimler Roadliners, the first motorbuses in the fleet which were not Gardner-powered. Twelve were delivered in 1967, but a repeat order for 12 was quickly changed to single-deck Fleetlines — and reverted to Gardner engines.

Above:
Sunderland Corporation was committed to one-man buses with a zonal fare system inspired by continental European practices. Its standard bus was the Strachans-bodied Leyland Panther, but it also ran 10 outwardly similar Bristol RELL6Gs with Metro-Cammell bodies. An RE leads a Panther through the town centre.

Among late deliveries of AEC Swifts were a batch of 18 with Marshall bodies which were ordered by Sunderland, but were delivered in 1973-74 to the expanded Tyne & Wear PTE.

Single-deck Fleetlines served Darlington — and a number of other operators — altogether better than had the Roadliners. This 1972 Roe-bodied SRG-series Fleetline gave Darlington over 20 years' service.

By common consent the most successful of the early rear-engined models was Bristol's RE. Its layout was different from its competitors in that the gearbox was mounted ahead of the rear axle rather than between the axle and the engine. It became popular not only with NBC companies, but with many municipal fleets too. Most had Gardner engines, but this Ribble bus is a Leyland-powered RESL6L. It is seen in Windermere in 1987. A Leyland National, the bus which killed off the RE, lurks behind the Atlantean.

In the Middle East, Egyptian and Israeli troops were fighting for control of the Gaza Strip and, in America, a freak snowstorm brought down power-lines and closed many roads in the North Eastern states. Back home, chip shop owners were growing concerned that the severe potato shortage would cause the price of a bag of chips to rise to 5d.

And in Sheffield, at ten past three in the morning, the 95 was born.

This new bus service, a six-mile cross-city route linking Walkley and Intake, was a direct replacement for the trams which had been withdrawn at the end of the previous day's operation; indeed, the first bus to Intake ran just about an hour and a half after the last tram.

This had been Sheffield's first tram route to go for two years, but the replacement programme subsequently gathered pace with closures following every six months or so until the final route succumbed in October 1960.

The Walkley route was one of the first electric tram routes in Sheffield, although the area had previously been served by horse buses and, for a few months prior to electrification, by horse trams.

In 1872, a horse bus service was introduced between the city and the Springvale Hotel at Steel Bank (Commonside). This ran via Upperthorpe but was never really profitable and was abandoned by 1882. New houses were being built in Walkley and a company was formed to recommence the service in 1883; a second route was added in 1884 linking the city and Springvale by way of Western Bank.

However, it was in 1886 that the Upperthorpe, Steel Bank and Walkley Omnibus Company bought its third bus and introduced what was to become the basis of the present 95 route. Their third – and final – route ran from Fitzalan Square to Harcourt Road via West Street and Brook Hill, passing the Fever Hospital on Winter Street before crossing the recently-constructed 'new Dam road' through Crookes Valley.

Meanwhile, horse trams had been working in the city since 1873 when the Attercliffe route had been inaugurated; by 1896, when they were acquired by the Corporation, five routes were in operation.

The Corporation soon came under pressure from a local residents' group demanding a line to Walkley. Their representations were eventually successful and a horse tram service to Harcourt Road began on 8 November 1898, the route chosen being similar to that of the horse buses although the trams went via Hounsfield Road. Two cars provided a 20-minute service with fares of 2d up and 1d down.

95 in '95

What could be more appropriate in 1995 than to look at a route 95. **Daniel Hill** traces the history of a Sheffield bus route which has survived with little change for almost 40 years.

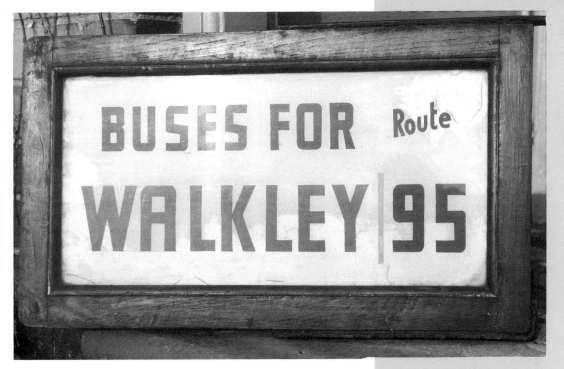

Above:
The tramway era, with Sheffield's appropriately-numbered tram 95 passing Walkley Ebenezer Church on its way to the city centre in August 1955. The 61-seat Corporation-built tram was new in 1932.
A. D. PACKER

Bottom:
Sheffield was unusual in having AEC Regent IIIs with concealed radiators. One of the batch ordered for the Walkley to Intake tram conversion waits to depart from Elm Tree for South Road. A. B. CROSS

Neither Leyland Titans nor exposed radiators were familiar sights on the 95. A 1953 Weymann-bodied PD2/12 carries a good load as it climbs Duke Street on an Elm Tree short-working.
R. F. MACK

Beyond Harcourt Road, the terrain becomes much more severe with steep gradients (up to 1 in 10 in places) and sharp curves; consequently, when the tram tracks had been laid up Barber Road and past Commonside, the Board of Trade inspector recommended a longer period of driver training. As a result, the introduction of electric trams through to South Road was delayed a fortnight and public service began at 7am on Monday, 18 September 1899 with the route initially restricted to single-deck cars only. A 12-minute service was provided but demand was so great that the horse cars had to be put back in service to help out. Fares were reduced to 1d all the way, and a half-penny as far as Harcourt Road.

Trams were introduced on the Intake section on 10 January 1990 – electric cars right from the start – with single-decker number 41, a new 28-seater, inaugurating the 20-minute service to Manor Lane, a short distance below the City Road Cemetery. In April 1902 the service was extended beyond the city boundary at Elm Tree (Manor Top) to Woodhouse Road in what was then Handsworth Urban District Council territory. A horse bus service between the city and Intake village, which had begun in 1898, was soon abandoned.

The through service linking Walkley and Intake was introduced in January 1903 although short workings between the city and Springvale continued. The last extensions to the route took place in 1935, the Intake terminus moving to Hollinsend Road in February and finally the short distance to Birley Vale on 29 December. By this time, a basic four minute service was in operation.

Trams were withdrawn from the route on Saturday, 7 April 1956. The last journey to Walkley ran at 11.30pm with car 55, one of the city's oldest – a 68-seat Brush car of 1925 vintage. At the South Road terminus a crowd of almost 200 had gathered and many souvenir pennies were crushed under the tram's wheels. One of the newest trams – car 505, a 64-seat Roberts car just six years old – worked the last trip to Intake at 1.30am on Sunday morning with eight enthusiasts having taken a final ride on both trams.

The 95 bus service was to be operated by Leadmill Road Garage; the route was the same as the trams except that the buses omitted Hounsfield Road, which was to be closed for extensions to the University. A new bus station was constructed alongside the tram terminus at Intake, whereas the Walkley terminus was moved to Tinker Lane, an extension of just over half a mile, taking buses past the old quarries on Bolehill Road. A basic 10min service was provided (eight-minute service on Saturdays) with extra buses running between the old South Road Library terminus and Elm Tree.

Middle:
AEC Bridgemaster demonstrator 60MMD spent a week in Sheffield in July 1957. Its duties included runs on the 95. It is seen at the Intake terminus.
DANIEL HILL COLLECTION

Bottom:
The 20 Alexander-bodied Regent Vs delivered in 1960 were regular performers on the 95. One leaves Commercial Street on a short-working to Commonside in August 1973.
P. HANWELL

New works services were also introduced between Walkley and the industrial East End – the 195 to Vulcan Road and the 295 serving Brightside. These were subsequently renumbered 195/196 then later 795/796 before they were withdrawn altogether during the 1980s due to the closure of many of the factories they served. Special trams between Intake and the East End continued for a further six months before being replaced by buses.

In preparation for the route conversion, the Transport Department had ordered 45 new Weymann-bodied 58-seaters; originally Leyland Titans had been specified but the order was changed in favour of AEC Regent IIIs at a cost of around £4,300 each. However, to ensure that sufficient vehicles would be available for the changeover, it had been agreed to divert nine Roe-bodied Regent IIIs which had been destined for the Joint Omnibus Committee for use on the new route; subsequently, nine of the Weymann-bodied AECs would be supplied as lowbridge vehicles for the JOC in lieu.

The Roe-bodied Regents (type 9613S with 58-seat bodies) became 736 to 744 (VWJ 536-44) and all but 743/4 entered service on the first day of the 95, the other two following the next day. The Weymann-bodied examples (also 9613S but 58-seaters) were 745 to 780 (WWB 745-80) but only 16 were available for 8 April, another half-dozen arriving by the end of the month. For the first eight or nine years of its existence,

Left:
Works service 195 served the Vulcan Road factories. The return journey on an August afternoon in 1973 was in the hands of a Roe-bodied PD3.
P. HANWELL

Top:
The batch of 25 Park Royal-bodied Fleetlines delivered in 1964 served the 95 from then until 1982. This one, No 112, seen in Commercial Street in 1968, was to become the last survivor. It was the oldest bus in the PTE fleet when it worked its final afternoon on the 95 on 13 March 1982.

Below:
A stranger in the camp! The 1990 Christmas and New Year operations were put out to tender and SUT/Sheaf Line won the contract for the 95. One of Sheaf Line's two Neoplans is seen on the route on New Year's Day 1991.
DANIEL HILL

Above:
The DMS-style Fleetlines served the 95 from their arrival in 1977. One crosses Fitzalan Square.
DANIEL HILL

the 95 was served almost exclusively by concealed-radiator Regents, the original 27-footers being joined in 1960 by 30-foot long Mark Vs with both Weymann and Alexander 69-seat bodies.

In December 1964, the first five of an order for 25 Park Royal-bodied Daimler Fleetlines arrived; these were 101-105 (DWJ 301-5B). The remainder arrived during January and February 1965, registered EWB 106-125C. This batch entered service on the 95 and served the route faithfully throughout their career; they were later joined by sister vehicles 964-966 (AWB 964-6B). When Townhead Street Garage closed in March 1968, a batch of 20 East Lancs-bodied Leyland Atlanteans was transferred in its entirety to Leadmill Road; numbered 162-181 (KWJ 162-81D), these were to operate on the 95 alongside the Fleetlines. For some years, these two types worked the majority of duties on the route, replacing – but never completely ousting – the Regents, which continued to see service in the peak hours.

During the early 1970s, Regents staged a comeback on the 95 with both 58- and 69-seaters in service during the week and the larger vehicles on Sundays. However, time was running out for the back-loaders and withdrawals were gradually reducing their numbers until the inevitable happened on 30 December 1976. The final day of service saw two

Regent Vs on the 95; Alexander-bodied 878 worked most of the day whilst Weymann-bodied 439 came out for the evening peak and became the last rear loader to work in service. By this time, the 95 was in the hands of South Yorkshire PTE, which had taken over Sheffield's operations on 1 April 1974.

Through the latter years of the 1970s and the early 1980s, most of Leadmill's vehicle types found their way on to the 95. Elderly MCW Atlanteans were later joined by Neepsend-bodied examples together with newer Park Royal Atlanteans and Fleetlines.

Silver Jubilee Year 1977 saw the arrival of a batch of new Fleetlines with MCW bodies to the London DMS style; 1501-1529 became regular performers on the route. Inter-garage transfers introduced Alexander-bodied Fleetlines of the NWA-K batch and SWB-L Atlanteans during 1979 and these served the route for around five years; a few ECW Fleetlines later added yet another style of bodywork.

In 1980, the first Metrobuses joined the South Yorkshire fleet and this type has operated on the route ever since, both single and dual door Mark I versions as well as the later Mark IIs.

As if there were not already enough vehicular variety, additional interest was provided by the involvement of Herries garage. For several years, a number of duties were transferred from Leadmill and worked by typical Herries vehicles including AN68 Atlanteans and, perhaps the most unusual types, some of the Van Hool-bodied Ailsas.

During 1981/2, various problems conspired to cause a shortage of serviceable vehicles and the PTE

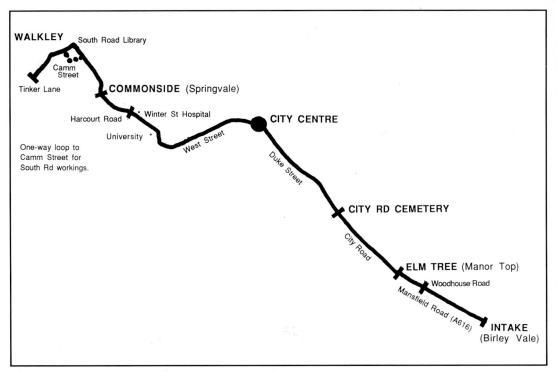

WALKLEY

South Road Library

Camm Street

Tinker Lane

COMMONSIDE (Springvale)

Winter St Hospital

Harcourt Road

University

West Street

One-way loop to Camm Street for South Rd workings.

CITY CENTRE

Duke Street

CITY RD CEMETERY

City Road

ELM TREE (Manor Top)

Woodhouse Road

Mansfield Road (A616)

INTAKE (Birley Vale)

Below:
Metrobuses have worked the route since 1980. A Mark 2, in obsolete Fastline livery, stands at Tinker Lane terminus in September 1993.   DANIEL HILL

had to hire in numerous vehicles from a variety of sources. Some routes were almost entirely given over to hired vehicles, but a few 'guest appearances' were made on the 95. In the spring of 1981, some ex-United Auto Bristol VRs were seen and in the 1981/2 winter, a couple of Greater Manchester Fleetlines made the odd foray on to the route.

These were not the first strangers in the camp, as the hilly route has been used to test a number of demonstrators. Way back in July 1957, AEC Bridgemaster 60 MMD was tried out for a week – and six were subsequently purchased. In 1971, two Bristol VRs were on loan – Lincolnshire Road Car 1909 (LFE 834H) for three days in October and East Midland's first VR, D101 (HAL 101K), for five days in November/December. Again, an order followed for 18 chassis, albeit with East Lancs bodies. During June and July 1977, London's DMS2224 (OJD 224R) was borrowed for evaluation of its hydraulic braking system.

The 95 was one of Sheffield's last crew-operated routes, the conversion to single-manning taking place on 6 April 1986. The Walkley terminus had been moved a short distance up Tinker Lane to avoid what had always been an awkward reverse manoeuvre; South Road workings had already ceased some seven years previously. By this time, the route was basically operated by Metrobuses and Fleetlines (ECW, Alexander and DMS-style varieties) but, after deregulation in October 1986, Metrobuses were generally the only vehicles allocated to the route.

Since deregulation, a host of new operators have started up to challenge South Yorkshire Transport's dominant position. The 95 saw some competition from Yorkshire Terrier for six months in 1988/9 when it began circular services 15/16 linking the City, Walkley and Crookes; SYT responded with short-lived minibus services M52 and M95. More recently, Yorkshire Terrier services 120/123 and South Riding's 46 have brought new competition and some fare wars to the route. However, only Andrews have regularly operated vehicles displaying the 95 route number; since 1991 they have worked two trips on the route as positioning journeys for a school contract.

At the time of writing, the 95 service is still one of the most frequent in the city, serving the University and several residential and shopping areas. The route has remained virtually unchanged since 1956 although roadworks for the Supertram have caused some diversions, as have various city centre traffic management schemes which currently take Intake-bound buses on a 1.5-mile tour of the city centre in order to avoid High Street.

Mainline, as successor to South Yorkshire Transport, provides a six-minute service Monday to Saturday using 15 vehicles – on Sundays, nine buses give a 20min headway. The route continues to be worked by Leadmill garage using a mixture of Mark II Metrobuses and Dennis Dominators and, despite an annual fall of some 15%, carries an average of 60,000 passengers each week.

Below:
A Dennis Dominator in Mainline livery passes construction work for the Sheffield Supertram on City Road in November 1993. DANIEL HILL

MAINLINE *Save money with a Day Return Ticket!*

SYT

WALKLEY → SHEFFIELD → INTAKE
via Crookesmoor, Park Hill, Manor Top

95

Certain journeys on this service are operated with funding from South Yorkshire P.T.E. in order to provide the public with a comprehensive travel system.

Mondays to Fridays

Walkley, Tinker Lane	0500	0515	0530	0545	0600	0615	0630	0645	0700	0710	0716	0722	0728	0734	0740	0744	0750	0756	then
Walkley, Commonside	0506	0521	0536	0551	0606	0621	0636	0651	0706	0716	0722	0728	0734	0740	0746	0750	0756	0802	every
Sheffield, High Street	0516	0531	0546	0601	0616	0631	0646	0701	0716	0726	0732	0738	0744	0750	0756	0802	0808	0814	6
Sheffield, Commercial Street	0520	0535	0550	0605	0620	0635	0650	0705	0720	0730	0736	0742	0748	0754	0800	0806	0812	0818	mins.
Manor Top, Elm Tree	0534	0549	0604	0619	0634	0649	0704	0719	0734	0744	0750	0756	0802	0808	0814	0821	0827	0833	until
Intake, Mansfield Road/Birley Moor Road	0538	0553	0608	0623	0638	0653	0708	0723	0738	0748	0754	0800	0806	0812	0818	0825	0831	0837	

Walkley, Tinker Lane	1656	1702	1708	1714	1720	1726	1732	1738	1746	1756		06	16	26	36	46	56		2156
Walkley, Commonside	1702	1708	1714	1720	1726	1732	1738	1744	1752	1802	then	12	22	32	42	52	02		2202
Sheffield, High Street	1714	1720	1726	1732	1738	1744	1750	1756	1803	1812	at	22	32	42	52	02	12		2212
Sheffield, Commercial Street	1718	1724	1730	1736	1742	1748	1754	1800	1807	1816	these	26	36	46	56	06	16	until	2216
Manor Top, Elm Tree	1733	1739	1745	1751	1757	1803	1808	1814	1821	1830	times	40	50	00	10	20	30		2230
Intake, Mansfield Road/Birley Moor Road	1737	1743	1749	1755	1801	1807	1812	1818	1825	1834		44	54	04	14	24	34		2234

Walkley, Tinker Lane	2206	2216	2226	2236	2246	2300	2306		
Walkley, Commonside	2212	2222	2232	2242	2252	2306	2312		
Sheffield, High Street	2222	2232	2242	2252	2302	2316	2322		
Sheffield, Commercial Street	2226	2236	2246	2256	2306	2317	—		
Manor Top, Elm Tree	2240	2250	2300	2310	2320	2331	—		
Intake, Mansfield Road/Birley Moor Road	2244	2254	2304	2314	2324	2335	—		

Intake, Mansfield Road/Birley Moor Road	0500	0520	0540	0600	0620	0630	0640	0650	0701	0707	0713	0719	0725	0731	0737	0741	0747	0753	0759
Manor Top, City Road	0504	0524	0544	0604	0624	0634	0644	0654	0705	0711	0717	0723	0729	0735	0741	0745	0751	0757	0803
Sheffield, Commercial Street	0519	0539	0559	0619	0639	0649	0659	0709	0720	0726	0732	0738	0744	0750	0756	0802	0808	0814	0820
Walkley, Commonside	0531	0551	0611	0631	0651	0701	0711	0721	0732	0738	0744	0750	0756	0802	0808	0814	0821	0828	0834
Walkley, Tinker Lane	0537	0557	0617	0637	0657	0707	0717	0727	0738	0744	0750	0756	0802	0808	0814	0820	0827	0834	0840

																			A
Intake, Mansfield Road/Birley Moor Road	then	1705	1711	1717	1723	1729	1736	1746	1756		06	16	26	36	46	56		2256	2306
Manor Top, City Road	every	1709	1715	1721	1727	1733	1740	1750	1800	then	10	20	30	40	50	00		2300	2310
Sheffield, Commercial Street	6	1726	1732	1738	1744	1750	1755	1805	1815	at	25	35	45	55	05	15	until	2315	2322
Walkley, Commonside	mins.	1740	1746	1752	1758	1803	1809	1817	1827	these	37	47	57	07	17	27		2327	—
Walkley, Tinker Lane	until	1746	1752	1758	1804	1809	1815	1823	1833	times	43	53	03	13	23	33		2333	—

Saturdays

Walkley, Tinker Lane	0516	0546	0616	0646	0716	0726	0736	0746	0756	0806	0816	0826	0836	0846	0856		1726	1732	1738
Walkley, Commonside	0522	0552	0622	0652	0722	0732	0742	0752	0802	0812	0822	0832	0842	0852	0902	then	1732	1738	1744
Sheffield, High Street	0532	0602	0632	0702	0732	0742	0752	0803	0814	0824	0834	0844	0854	0904	0914	every	1744	1750	1756
Sheffield, Commercial Street	0536	0606	0636	0706	0736	0746	0756	0807	0818	0828	0838	0848	0858	0908	0918	6	1748	1754	1803
Manor Top, Elm Tree	0550	0620	0650	0720	0750	0800	0811	0822	0833	0843	0853	0903	0913	0923	0933	mins.	1803	1808	1814
Intake, Mansfield Road/Birley Moor Road	0554	0624	0654	0724	0754	0804	0815	0826	0837	0847	0857	0907	0917	0927	0937	until	1807	1812	1818

Walkley, Tinker Lane	1746	1756		06	16	26	36	46	56		2156	2206	2216	2226	2236	2246	2300	2306
Walkley, Commonside	1752	1802	then	12	22	32	42	52	02		2202	2212	2222	2232	2242	2252	2306	2312
Sheffield, High Street	1803	1812	at	22	32	42	52	02	12		2212	2222	2232	2242	2252	2302	2316	2322
Sheffield, Commercial Street	1807	1816	these	26	36	46	56	06	16	until	2216	2226	2236	2246	2256	2306	2317	—
Manor Top, Elm Tree	1820	1830	times	40	50	00	10	20	30		2230	2240	2250	2300	2310	2320	2331	—
Intake, Mansfield Road/Birley Moor Road	1824	1834		44	54	04	14	24	34		2234	2244	2254	2304	2314	2324	2335	—

Intake, Mansfield Road/Birley Moor Road	0505	0535	0605	0635	0705	0716	0726	0736	0746	0756	0806	0816	0826	0836	0846	0853	0859	then	1705
Manor Top, City Road	0509	0539	0609	0639	0709	0720	0730	0740	0750	0800	0810	0820	0830	0840	0850	0857	0903	every	1709
Sheffield, Commercial Street	0524	0554	0624	0654	0724	0735	0745	0755	0806	0815	0825	0835	0847	0855	0907	0914	0920	6	1726
Walkley, Commonside	0536	0606	0636	0706	0736	0747	0757	0808	0820	0831	0841	0851	0901	0911	0921	0928	0934	mins.	1740
Walkley, Tinker Lane	0542	0612	0642	0712	0742	0753	0803	0814	0826	0837	0847	0857	0907	0917	0927	0934	0940	until	1746

															A
Intake, Mansfield Road/Birley Moor Road	1711	1717	1723	1729	1735	1746	1756		06	16	26	36	46	56		2256	2306
Manor Top, City Road	1715	1721	1727	1733	1739	1750	1800	then	10	20	30	40	50	00		2300	2310
Sheffield, Commercial Street	1732	1738	1744	1750	1756	1806	1815	at	25	35	45	55	05	15	until	2315	2322
Walkley, Commonside	1746	1752	1758	1803	1808	1818	1827	these	37	47	57	07	17	27		2327	—
Walkley, Tinker Lane	1752	1758	1804	1809	1814	1824	1833	times	43	53	03	13	23	33		2333	—

Sundays

Walkley, Tinker Lane	0516	0546		16	46		1046		06	26	46		2246	—	2306
Walkley, Commonside	0522	0552	then	22	52		1052	then	12	32	52		2252	—	2312
Sheffield, High Street	0532	0602	at	32	02		1102	at	22	42	02		2302	2315	2322
Sheffield, Commercial Street	0536	0606	these	36	06	until	1106	these	26	46	06	until	2306	2316	—
Manor Top, Elm Tree	0550	0620	times	50	20		1120	times	40	00	20		2320	2330	—
Intake, Mansfield Road/Birley Moor Road	0554	0624		54	24		1124		44	04	24		2324	2334	—

																	A
Intake, Mansfield Road/Birley Moor Road	0501	0531		01	31		0931	1001	1026	1046		06	26	46		2246	2306
Manor Top, City Road	0505	0535	then	05	35		0935	1005	1030	1050	then	10	30	50		2250	2310
Sheffield, Commercial Street	0520	0550	at	20	50	until	950	1020	1045	1105	at	25	45	05	until	2305	2322
Walkley, Commonside	0532	0602	these	32	02		1002	1032	1057	1117	these	37	57	17		2317	—
Walkley, Tinker Lane	0538	0608	times	38	08		1008	1038	1103	1123	times	43	03	23		2323	—

NOTE: A — Runs to Sheffield. Church Street arrives 2323.

Above:
This Volvo B10M with Duple Caribbean body started life with Walkers of Anderton as B637 LJU. Registration 716 GRM — coincidentally the photographer's initials — was transferred from an ex-Cumberland Lodekka owned by Walkers. It is seen at Wembley Stadium in 1989.
ALL PHOTOGRAPHS BY THE AUTHOR

WHAT'S IN A NUMBER?

More and more operators are using cherished registration numbers to either disguise the ages of their coaches or add a distinctive touch. **Geoff Mills** has been on the number trail.

Previous page bottom:
Originally LCN 834K, this former Northern General Plaxton-bodied Leopard carries a WHT registration mark for Waterhouse Tours of Polegate who were running it in 1989.

Top:
The distinctive styling of the Spanish-built Ayatts Diana makes it hard to date. This coach, based on Magirus Deutz running units, was in fact new to Little of Annan as ESW 717Y. Ulster registrations such as JXI 9142 are popular because they are relatively cheap to buy. This rare coach was owned by Richardson (Visionline) of Stevenage when photographed at Wembley in 1991.

Below:
Change the spacing on an Ulster number and it can look like a British registration. This former Green Line Leyland Tiger, originally YPD 137Y, carries an Omagh GJI mark, and not a London GJ as a quick glance would suggest. It is seen at South Mimms services on the M25 in 1991, owned by Ludlows of Halesowen.

Top:
An appropriate DD — for double-deck — registration is carried by this London Pride MCW Metroliner seen on tour in London's Whitehall in 1993. It started life in 1986 as C757 CWX.

Above:
This 1984 Leyland Tiger of Holmeswood Coaches of Ormskirk was originally Ribble's ANA 106Y. The registration which it was carrying in the summer of 1993, 201 SC, was issued 30 years earlier to an Edinburgh Corporation Bedford VAS coach.

Above and below:
Owners of an unusual registration will often transfer it between vehicles, as illustrated by Partridge of Hadleigh with 129 SDV. It is seen in 1988 on a Bedford VAS1 which was new in 1976 as LPB 116P and again in 1990 on a rather larger bus in the shape of an ex-Strathclyde Atlantean which was originally GGG 306N.

Top:
The most apt mark of all? Rover Bus of Chesham ran this Bedford YMT for a time with the registration 760 BUS. It was originally D620 PWA. It has a Plaxton Derwent bus body.

Above:
The operator's initials form the registration of this Plaxton-bodied Ford R1114 in the Peter Sheffield fleet, which was owned by Grimsby Cleethorpes Transport when this photograph was taken in 1990. The Ford started life with Anderson of Halifax in 1981 as LCX 566W.

Above:
SAB for Sabre. The unique ECW-bodied AEC Sabre coach operated by Kent-based Kemp's started life as CBU 636J. It is seen at Nottingham's Wollaton Park in 1990, attending an AEC rally.

Below:
Registrations in the SU and SV series are intended primarily for issue to older vehicles, although a number have found their way on to modern coaches, such as this Setra of Boon's of Boreham. The KSU letters conveniently stand for Kassbohrer Setra, Ulm — Ulm being the location of the Kassbohrer factory.

Top:
Numbers with year prefixes can be used to spell messages, such as H15 URE — HI SURE — of Harry Shaw of Coventry. The coach is a Volvo B10MT with Jonckheere body.

Above:
K90 EBL was delivered to Eastbourne Buses Limited in the 90th year of local authority-owned bus operation in the town. The year was 1993; the bus is a Dennis Lance with Wadham Stringer Vanguard body.

Fond Memories ...

In 1967 when this scene was captured, the Llandudno UDC bus fleet still wore a maroon and cream livery, unchanged from before World War 2. A long-standing tradition with holidaymakers in the town was to visit the open-air Sunday morning service at St Tudno's Church, high up on Great Ormes head. The very fit climbed up, whilst many made the journey by buses which waited for their return after the service. Sometimes the entire Llandudno fleet, at its peak eight small Guys and two 35-seat Fodens, was employed. Seen here are seven Guys; a Roe-bodied Otter of 1954 stands nearest the camera.
ALL PHOTOGRAPHS BY THE AUTHOR

Wirral-based **Reg Wilson** selects and comments on a few of his favourite photographs, covering a time span approaching 50 years.

Above:

Like most established bus fleets, Manchester's was at its largest in the 1950s and Parrs Wood depot at East Didsbury, seen here in 1950, had a yard equipped with steam heating to hold those buses which could not be accommodated inside the depot building. Prewar Crossleys and Leylands can be seen, together with one or two postwar Crossleys. All have regrettably lost their streamlined livery. The Leyland Tiger in the foreground was one of eight new in 1938-39 which were converted to airport coaches between 1946 and 1950 and stood out from the rest of the fleet in their dark blue and cream livery. Manchester's buses were red.

Below:

Ramsey bus station in the north of the Isle of Man still looks much like this, although the buses depicted in this May 1964 view have long since vanished. The livery, fleetname and ownership of the island's main operator have changed more than once in the intervening years although the colours have now reverted to the bright red and cream of 30 years ago. Seen here from left to right are a Leyland Olympic of 1950 standing inside the building, a Bedford OWB of 1945, a Leyland Titan PD1 built in 1946 and a Leyland Tiger PS1 of 1947 bodied, unusually, by ECW. Present-day occupants of the bus station are mainly Nationals, Olympians and Darts. Isle of Man Road Services originally had links with Cumberland Motor Services, whose territory is often in sight less than 40 miles away. It is now part of the Manx national transport organisation

Above:
An action shot of a classic bus, my favourite angle which shows most features. This was taken in June 1960 in Hove, during a family holiday on the south coast. The vehicle is a Brighton Corporation AEC Regent III with 56-seat Weymann body. Built in 1950, it was one of a batch of six. Our Ford car of that time is also in the photo. It got us there and back from the northwest using the newly-opened and nearly deserted M1 at a steady 40mph.

Right:
The coach may be far from home but the registration, transferred from a Routemaster, certainly isn't as Western Scottish H107, a Duple 425 Integral proceeds from Whitehall into Parliament Square, London. The coach, photographed in May 1990, looked very smart in white, grey, black and red.

Above:

For much of its lower course the River Dee forms the boundary between Wales and England. One of the many interesting crossings is this old narrow bridge joining the twin villages of Holt in Clwyd with Farndon in Cheshire. A Crosville Lodekka on route C56, Chester-Wrexham, passes into Wales whilst pedestrians use a refuge, one of several formed by the bridge buttresses. Although over 25 miles from the open Irish Sea, the Dee at the bridge is still tidal and I have recollections as an eight-year-old of floating in my uncle's rowing boat up to the bridge on the flood and, after shopping in Farndon, floating back down on the ebb to his riverside home in a converted railway carriage. This view was taken many years later, in February 1966.

Below:

On 1 August 1969 a Daimler Fleetline CRG6LX with Northern Counties 74-seat body was loaded on to MV Clan Maclean from Lewis's Quay adjacent to Poulton Bridge on the Wallasey side of Wirral's Great Float dock system. Having been new to Halifax in 1968 it was reacquired by Daimler to go to South Africa as a demonstrator. It entered service with City Tramways in Cape Town and remained there until being scrapped in 1977. I was lucky to have seen the preparation for loading and was therefore on hand when the bus went skyward. This view is one of a series I took on that occasion. The background buildings were flour mills on the Birkenhead side of the Float and were demolished in the early 1990s.

Top:
This wasn't taken as a bus view, but was recognised as having such potential in later years. Shot from Richmond Castle, North Yorkshire, it captures the informal parking arrangements for buses and cars in most country towns in the early 1950s. The date is July 1953 and the occasion a cycling tour of the Yorkshire Dales. Richmond is still a wonderful place despite parking problems and still sees United Automobile buses, but not, unfortunately, the prewar type of Bristol/ECW shown here.

Above:
Kirkstone Pass in Cumbria is the most direct way from Penrith to Ambleside and Windermere. It is, therefore, used by many coaches such as the Midland Red example seen here heading south towards the summit in June 1963. The chassis, a BMMO type C3, was nine years old at the time, but the Plaxton Panorama body had been fitted in 1962, extending the coach's front-line service life. The livery was red and black with a cream band, considerably brighter than the company's bus livery.

The peninsula of Wirral (incorrectly referred to by many as The Wirral) is a dichotomy, the east being industrial and built-up; the west smaller towns, seaside and open country with views across the Dee to Wales. The village of Caldy is one of the gems on the west side and was served by Crosville for half a century until the effects of deregulation compelled a change to a smaller operator. Here in more predictable times — April 1984 — is a Crosville Leyland Olympian, then less than one year old, which passed to Midland Red North in the 'great carve-up'. It is passing the church hall, well known as a hazard to upper decks. Route 80 ran from West Kirby to Birkenhead Woodside. Crosville, now a PMT look-alike, still serves Caldy, but not the village centre.

Left:
In 1975 my wife and I treated ourselves to a Silver Wedding trip to southern Africa to visit relatives and one of the marvellous places we toured was the Royal Natal National Park, nestling beneath the enormous cliffs of the Drakensbergs — Dragon Mountains — the peaks of which at that point are the border with independent Lesotho, until 1966 the British Protectorate of Basutoland. Public transport in that part of Natal was then run by South African Railways using dark red and cream buses, some of them articulated tractor/trailer type such as this International Harvester. The bus is near Bergville.

Left:
In 1984 Western Scottish ran an outpost on the island of Islay off the west coast of Scotland and a small fleet of dual-purpose vehicles bore a special fleetname — Islay Western Scottish. From Bowmore, the island capital, they operated local, cross-island and school services and connected with ferries from the mainland to Port Ellen and Port Askaig. One route ran from Bowmore to Portnahaven, a picturesque fishing village at the end of the peninsula called Rinns of Islay. The terminus was above the horseshoe-shaped village, one side of which can be seen here. This Duple Dominant-bodied Leyland Leopard with bus seats was new to Paton Bros of Renfrew. Livery was the then standard Western red and cream.

Left:
On 27 July 1984 the public were allowed to tour the Royal Liver Building on Liverpool's waterfront and this provided a rare opportunity for a high view of what was then the Pier Head bus station. The buses shown are all Merseyside PTE except one Crosville (top left) with a yellow front for the Garden Festival service. Only one, a National, is single-decked. In the last year or two the area shown, after a brief revamp to provide more lay-over parking, has been cleared of public transport and is now being made into an attractive piazza.

Never Too Late

The British Bus Preservation Group has secured the future of more than 50 historic buses and coaches since its formation in 1990. Founder and chairman **Nick Larkin** reveals the secrets behind the BBPG's formation, and looks at the group today.

It may have all resulted from a blow on the head in Stockton-on-Tees High Street, circa 1965. On a visit to the North East as a mere toddler, the opportunity of riding on a dark green Corporation Leyland PD2 had consumed me with frenzied excitement. When the bus shuddered to a halt I bounded excitedly off the platform, unfortunately failing to notice a large litter bin. The result? A visit to the local hospital.

This incident has been blamed for knocking into me a passion for buses and coaches which has remained undimmed and undaunted ever since.

It can also be said to be at least partly to blame for the formation of the British Bus Preservation Group 25 years or so later, along with another personal trauma.

Just into my teenage years, I was standing in Hartlepool Corporation's depot yard looking wistfully at the operator's last Roe-bodied exposed radiator Daimler CVG6, AEF 593, just out of service after 22 years. The polished interior woodwork still shone, and had a smell only aged moquette can create; mingling with the oily mechanical odour of a well-used psv.

The whole bus had the aura of an elderly public servant, its work done; a slightly battered warrior after its last battle. Surely this veteran deserved a secure future where its magical fluid flywheel-inspired engine notes could thrill future generations.

But it wasn't to be. My personal crusade to save it had failed, after no one with any authority had taken a

Below:
Remarkable survivor: this prewar Bristol K was rescued from a garden in Suffolk.
NICK LARKIN

Above:
Albion aid: the ex-Red & White Albion is lifted on to a low-loader after 30 years out of use.
TONY BREWIN

blind bit of notice, and AEF 593 suddenly disappeared, leaving me with a sense of outrage, frustration and pure helplessness.

As the 1970s progressed, my favourite Southdown Guys became just a memory; like Eastbourne AECs and Northern Routemasters not long afterwards they were replaced by Portakabins on wheels with aggressive sounding engines and nasty vinyl interiors. Just as I thought all was completely lost, I discovered Buses magazine, and Buses Annual (I still have my original copy from 1970) but it was not until 1988 that I finally joined the ranks of preservationists, with the Number 7 Bus Preservation Group to secure the future of former Pontypridd/Taff Ely AEC Regent V UTG 312G.

Like so many before us, we soon discovered just how monumental was the task of preserving and restoring a real double-decker, particularly in dealing with the biggest burden of all – finding accommodation.

We met many other enthusiasts with similar or worse problems, battling to keep a vehicle against the overwhelming odds of the elements and vandalism with no support from anyone. Sometimes these and other unexpected horrors had meant they'd either lost interest or merely been forced to send a vehicle for scrap, not knowing anyone who might want to save it.

All this contributed to so many of those psvs listed in Buses as having been sold for preservation over the past 20 or so years no longer being with us, even if they'd once been repainted and rallied frequently.

In 1990, many interesting halfcabs were still in daily use as driver trainers, but new legislation would soon render them obsolete. Mass scrappings were on the cards.

This, coupled with the advancing recession, was further evidence that now, more than ever, a national organisation was needed to cater for committed bus and coach enthusiasts whether or not they owned vehicles; to act as a network to save interesting psvs in danger, and to tackle head on the problems of storage,

spares, legislation and every other blessed obstacle!

It was all these factors, plus the bitter memory of that lost West Hartlepool Daimler which pushed the normally lethargic me into action.

Having previously worked on Bus Business newspaper, I knew there were people in the industry prepared to back, and even join, such a group of people who were not bell-ringing bus spotters.

Talking to more people at rallies and tentative press publicity showed such an organisation could have massive support within the preservation movement. So, finally, following what I have been forced to admit was my non-stop ranting on the subject, the Number 7

Bus Preservation Group crossed its collective fingers, took a deep breath and formed the embryo British Bus Preservation Group.

The BBPG's inaugural meeting took place in September 1990, and today it has some 800 members including some of the best known names in preservation. We can justifiably claim to have secured the future of more than 50 buses and coaches, as different as a 1932 Leyland TD2 and a 1969 Alexander M-Type motorway coach.

Never for a moment would we say that running a group such as the BBPG has been easy. The sheer bulk of work involved, and covering completely new ground as a national group actually going out and rescuing interesting vehicles, meant that only the relentless encouragement and support from our new members, particularly in those difficult early days,

Below:
Modern machine: a Series 2 Bristol VR, still in service but earmarked for preservation.
NICK LARKIN

Above:
Southdown saved: a 1935 Titan, now under restoration.
NICK LARKIN

stopped the fledgling BBPG from falling flat on its face.

Fate had dealt us one or two other favours. A sympathetic printer saved our bacon producing the first ten issues of our bi-monthly magazine free of charge as his contribution to preservation, And secondly, we were offered a barn near Hull to store long-term restoration projects which would otherwise have been scrapped.

Membership soared, and we battled to keep up with the demand for BBPG information. Luckily, people were prepared to step in and help.

A highly important factor in the group's success has probably been our determination to remain a pomposity free but effective organisation, running on

Left:
Good Guy: a JCB hauls an ex-Gosport & Fareham Arab on to a trailer in Kent.
NICK LARKIN

as informal a basis as we possibly could, and making
every effort to avoid the personality clashes and petty
wranglings which affect so many groups, whether they
try to cater for the needs of bus enthusiasts or keepers
of tropical fish.

We have also tried to represent and act upon the
views of our members, partly through a series of
questionnaires. The general, though not the only,
consensus of opinion has been that the BBPG as a
group should concentrate on saving older and
historically important vehicles.

But people felt we should publicise details of every
known interesting vehicle for sale or in jeopardy. This
is done through our magazine, British Bus News,
which is crammed with articles on preservation, our

members' projects and their sales and wants.

Additionally, we issue a regular list of every
known available potential preservation candidate,
which is circulated free to people sending an SAE. In
exceptional cases, we circulate emergency news sheets
to members. The most successful of these resulted in
at least eight historic single-deckers, including 1953
Leyland Royal Tigers AEK 516 and NGY 576/7 being
saved when 24 similar vehicles latterly owned by
Phillips of Shiptonthorpe were sold to a breaker in
1993.

As much money as possible from subscriptions,
donations and fundraising goes into the BBPG Bus
Rescue Fund, though resources are severely limited.
We have rescued some vehicles from scrapyards,
raised cash deposits to secure others; and also paid
towards having significant vehicles towed from danger
to safe dry storage. The BBPG has also set up share
ownership schemes to secure individual vehicles, and
helped form groups of co-owners to look after them.

Possibly the most astonishing discovery which has
come to light since forming the BBPG is just how
many buses and coaches 30-years-old or more are still
around, usually out of the public eye, but often in
extreme jeopardy.

Who'd have thought, for example, that we would
find ourselves hiring a crane to winch a 1935 ex-Red
and White Albion Valiant, AAX 284, to safety on the
very morning it was due to be cut up so a portable
building could be put on the site it had occupied since
1961? Or we'd be dragging a 1942 ex-Provincial Guy
Arab, EHO 869, out of a yard with a borrowed JCB

113

two hours before a wrecking crew was due to move in?

There are many, many other deserving candidates still around, and the BBPG has a policy of never competing with any genuine preservationist in buying

a particular vehicle. We also try to pass on rescued vehicles to good homes, while trying to ensure they don't slip through the preservation net again.

We have managed to build up an excellent relationship with many of the Yorkshire bus breakers, having a 'scrapyard co-ordinator' who liaises on our behalf. We are also keeping a close eye on another well-known source of preservable vehicles, the Perthshire berry farmers; again, having a liaising representative.

As well as the rescue of vehicles, the BBPG tries within its limited resources to provide as many back-up services as possible.

The BBPG Storage Scheme lists sites across the country where vehicles can be stored, from large warehouses to single outdoor spaces; our Spares Scheme gives people the chance to list the parts they have for sale and those they need; and our Towing Scheme lists people prepared to transport vehicles at a discount. We also have trade plates available to members.

We are also doing our best to monitor legislation affecting PSV preservation, working closely with the Federation of British Historic Vehicle Clubs, which has sponsored a lobbyist in Brussels.

Recent major appeals are the BBPG Crossley Appeal, which aimed to rescue three Crossleys and other vehicles from a Cambridgeshire scrapyard; and the BBPG TD appeal to save three 1932 ex-Eastern Counties Leyland TD2s owned by a Norfolk breaker. Finally, the BBPG Building Appeal aims to raise funds for a low cost building in which further long-term restoration projects of great historical importance can be stored.

So, the BBPG has scored many successes, but there are still far more preservable vehicles around than people prepared to preserve them; fundraising is still a problem for the group and our original dream of housing a collection of representative buses and coaches in a National Museum is still a long way off.

We have no divine right to be able to save vehicles, and despite our efforts, some are still slipping through the net; most annoyingly in one or two cases after considerable efforts by the group to find homes for them.

In the immediate future the group is continuing to work hard to spread the psv preservation cause. Efforts are also to be aimed at making sure surviving film of long-lost vehicles is preserved by producing a series of videos.

So, the BBPG has at least made some progress in tackling major problems, though there's still a long way to go.

One of the questions we are most often asked is Why wasn't a group like the BBPG formed 20/30/40 years ago?' That's not for us to say, and to be honest, there's too much work in hand at the moment to waste our energies mourning buses which might have been saved.

But who can help but reflect on whether we could have still had with us vehicles such as that ex-West Hartlepool Daimler CVG6 whose loss eclipsed spots among my greatest teenage traumas; or even the Stockton PD, the charms of which resulted in an extremely sore head for one young passenger!

• If you'd like to know more about the BBPG, send an SAE to the membership secretary, Alan Shepherd, The Shieling, Forcett, Richmond, North Yorkshire, DL11 7RU. New members are always welcome!

Below:
Super Seven: the bus that started it all, a Taff-Ely Regent V
NICK LARKIN

Past Preservation

The roots of the present healthy bus preservation movement can be traced back to the 1950s. **Michael Fowler** turns the clock back 20 years and illustrates some of the vehicles on the rally scene in 1975.

Below:
Even in 1975 prewar preserved buses were relatively uncommon in rallies. One stalwart was ex-Portsmouth Leyland Titan TD4 RV 6367. New in 1935 it had English Electric bodywork. The 40-year-old Titan, which is still around, is seen in central Bradford.
ALL PHOTOGRAPHS BY THE AUTHOR

Previous page top right:
Dennis's small Dart achieved prominence in the 1990s, but an earlier generation of Dart is represented by this 1930s machine. It has Dennis bodywork and now resides in Bradford Industrial Museum. The cars which were following it near Shipley in 1975 are of more than passing interest 20 years later — a Ford Capri followed by a Hillman Imp.

Top left:
One of the first double-deckers to be preserved in Scotland was Alexander's AWG 393, an unusual combination of Guy Arab III chassis and Cravens body. It now lives at the Scottish Vintage Bus Museum.

Bottom left:
A contrast in Regents at Sandtoft: on the left an unusual single-deck Regent V which was new to South Wales Transport; on the right an ex-York Pullman Regent III. Both have bodywork by Charles H. Roe of Leeds. SWT bought single-deck Regents for operation under a bridge which was too low for underfloor-engined buses.

Top right:
Hayfield School in Doncaster rallied this Dennis Falcon with Duple body. It is seen heading through Auckley on its way to the Sandtoft Gathering. It was later scrapped.

Centre right:
The RT-type AEC Regents operated by St Helens Corporation looked particularly smart in the municipality's red and cream livery. BDJ 67 was new in 1950. It is now at the St Helens Transport Museum and is still rallied.

Below right:
Manchester's fleet is well-represented in the ranks of preserved buses. This is a 58-seat Metro-Cammell-bodied Daimler CVG6, new in 1950. It is pictured running through Otley.

Left:
A Midland Red own-build BMMO D7 photographed in central Otley. It was one of 350 similar buses bodied by Metro-Cammell and delivered between 1953 and 1957. This bus was new in 1955 and was taken out of service in 1972.

Right:
A relatively young preserved bus in 1975 was this ex-Brighton Hove & District Bristol Lodekka LDS6B which was new in 1959. It had 60-seat ECW bodywork.

Left:
Bus operator's service vehicles have also found their way into preservation. This 1939 AEC Regent from the Nottingham fleet was converted to a tower wagon after an accident in 1950. It was sold for preservation in 1970 and moved to Sandtoft, where this picture was taken, in the spring of 1975.

Above:
Change was afoot in London in 1985. Titans may still be around, but Poplar garage, location of this view, closed in November that year. The Titan in the foreground moved north to Merseybus in 1993. ALL PHOTOGRAPHS BY THE AUTHOR

Below right:
Three Dennis Dominators were on trial in London in 1985. Dennis went on to become London Buses' biggest supplier — but not of double-deckers. Northern Counties built the body.

Ten Years Ago

Depending on your age, 10 years can seem like an eternity — or the day before yesterday. **Kevin Lane** has delved into his negatives to see what he was photographing in 1985

Above:
Route tendering by London Regional Transport was getting under way. Eastern National, then part of the National Bus Company, gained a route in North London which it operated with unusual Wadham Stringer-bodied Bedfords. Ten years on NBC and Bedford have gone, while Wadham Stringer has changed hands and is now known simply as WS Coachbuilders.

Left:
Len Wright's London Buslines took over a tendered LRT route in West London in mid-year, running ex-London DMSs. One is seen in Hounslow.

Above:
Routemaster operation still stretched well out from central London, as illustrated by the long 109 service which worked south from the centre to Purley, where this bus is seen in January.

Below:
United Counties was still intact in 1985, although soon to be split into three companies. A Bristol RESL braves the snow in Dunstable, which became Luton & District territory.

Minibuses were beginning their rapid spread 10 years ago. Those for United Counties included Ford Transits — whose durability was to surprise even the most profound critics of minibus operation.

Below:
Swindon was in the middle of a period of remarkable growth, as the part-completed building in the background shows. The Thamesdown buses are a Fleetline and a rare single-deck Dominator.

Above:
Oxford was to become a hot-bed of minibus competition, but that was still in the future when this ex-Southend Fleetline in the City of Oxford fleet was loading in the city centre.

Opposite top:
Aberconwy ceased operating its stage service up the
Great Orme in 1985. Crosville took over, using a B-series
Leyland National.

Above:
The work of the Passenger Transport Executives in service
co-ordination was highly visible in Tyne & Wear, where
NBC buses wore a yellow livery to match those owned by
the PTE. A Northern General dual-door Bristol VRT makes
the point in South Shields.

Opposite left:
Unusual survivors in the London Country fleet were the
AEC Reliances bought secondhand from Barton
Transport. One stands in the central bus station at
Heathrow Airport.

Above:
By 1985 AEC Swifts were not quite as common as they had once been. A number survived in Blackpool. They had Marshall bodywork.